i.c. 3/16   12/13

D1193408

Holocaust

BY

GEORGE LEE

COPYRIGHT © 1998 Mark Twain Media, Inc.

ISBN   10-digit: 1-58037-070-5
           13-digit: 978-1-58037-070-7

Printing No. CD-1899

Mark Twain Media, Inc., Publishers
Distributed by Carson-Dellosa Publishing LLC

Visit us at www.carsondellosa.com

Table of Contents

Introduction

There is, hidden inside most of us, an evil attitude we call prejudice. It is a dark spirit that is usually quiet, but it may suddenly come roaring out when it spots someone it dislikes. This person may go to a rival school, be mentally or physically handicapped, speak with an accent or not speak our language at all, wear odd clothing, or have a different religion, nationality, or skin color. Prejudice concludes this person is somehow inferior, cannot be trusted, or is a threat.

Most of us know that prejudice should be caged, because it makes us feel guilty, goes against our religion or conscience, and leads to destructive acts. If none of these reasons cause us to cage it, we know it is illegal and will get us into trouble. If we allow prejudice to be released in words, we call it hate-talk or bigotry; if we act on it, we call it discrimination.

There was a time, not too many years ago, when prejudice was not only uncaged, but was allowed to roam freely across a continent. It targeted many humans: the deformed, retarded, political opponents, and groups it had decided to label "subhuman." Of all the groups it wanted to torment, the Jews were its main prey. At first, the beast was satisfied with humiliating its victims, destroying their property, and taking away their jobs and security. After 1942, it unleashed its full fury on the victims, hunting them down at night, rousting them from sleep, dragging them out to trucks, holding them in terror, and then taking them away in cattle cars. It allowed some to live, but it destroyed others.

What happened is a great tragedy in human history. It is the story of Nazi Germany and its leader, Adolf Hitler, who was determined to wipe Jews and other "subhumans" from the face of the earth. It is the story of victims caught in an unreal world of cattle cars, barbed wire, cruel guards, starvation, and death. It is also the story of brave people who risked their own lives by hiding the hunted and by helping them survive.

Unfortunately, it is a story that has been repeated since in the "Killing Fields" of Cambodia, tribal warfare in Rwanda, and "ethnic cleansing" in Bosnia. It warns each of us how dangerous our beast can be. It also comes with a warning to those who turn the beast loose and a promise to the victim.

Centuries ago, the prophet Jeremiah warned the enemies of Israel: "All who devour you shall be devoured, and all your foes, every one of them shall go into captivity; those who despoil you shall become a spoil, and all who prey on you I will make a prey. For I will restore health to you, and your wounds I will heal, says the Lord, because they have called you an outcast: 'It is Zion for whom no one cares!' Thus says the Lord: Behold, I will restore the fortunes of the tents of Jacob, and have compassion on his dwellings. ..." (Jer. 30:16–18 RSV)

— The Author

Terms

The following terms are used in the book, usually without definition. This list will help the reader understand their meaning. In the interest of space, their name in German has not been included.

Aktion—Gangs of anti-Semites formed to force Jews into labor camps. It is also used in reference to violence against Jews.

AMT VI—Office 6. Branch of RSHA responsible for the Final Solution; it was headed by Adolf Eichmann.

Anti-Semitism—Prejudice or hostility toward Jews.

Aryan—In Nazi terminology, the Master Race.

Block—Housing for prisoners, one-story brick or wooden buildings.

Block Senior—Prisoner appointed by the SS to be responsible for a block.

"Canada"—Large warehouses where confiscated prisoner property was stored.

Capo—Prisoner appointed by the SS to be foreman of a labor squad.

Concentration camp—Used by Nazis to hold anyone they regarded as an enemy. Inmates wore badges determining the category of their offense.

Confessional Church—Protestants refusing to accept Nazi religious doctrines.

DAP—German Worker's Party; original name for Nazi (NSDAP) party.

Death camp (extermination camp)—A camp existing primarily for the quick killing of prisoners.

Death wall (black wall)—Where firing squad executions took place.

Einsatzgruppen—Mobile units killing Jews in occupied lands.

Einsatzkommandos—Detachments of Einsatzgruppen units.

I.G. Farben—Major German corporation using many slave laborers.

Final Solution—Name given to the German goal of killing all European Jews.

Frei Korps—Fanatic German nationalists fighting Communists in street battles in the 1920s; most later joined the Nazi party.

German Faith Movement—Nazis' perverted version of Christianity.

Gestapo—Secret State police headed by Heinrich Himmler. Much feared by everyone in Germany because of their cruelty.

Ghetto—Section of city inhabited only by Jews.

Holocaust—Systematic slaughter of European Jews by the Nazis.

"Juda Verrecke!" (Death to Judaism)—A favorite Nazi slogan.

Judenfrei—Slogan meaning "Cleansed of Jews," used by Nazis after every Jew was either dead or removed from an area.

Judenrat—Jewish council formed by Germans as a way to issue orders to Jews and administer Jewish affairs.

Julag—Concentration camp with only Jewish inmates.

Kripo—Criminal police. Branch of the SD.

Kristallnacht (Night of the Broken Glass)—November 9, 1938, when mobs throughout Germany destroyed Jewish property and terrorized Jews.

KZ—Concentration camp.

Mischlenge—Those with mixed (Jewish and Gentile) blood.

"Moslems"—The "walking dead" of concentration camps who looked and acted like zombies.

Nazi—Common name for the NSDAP party.

NSDAP—National Socialist German Workers' Party. Proper name for the Nazi party.

Nuremberg Laws—1935 laws defining the status of Jews and withdrawing citizenship from persons of non-German blood.

OKH—High command of the German army.

OKW—High command of the armed forces.

Ordo—Uniformed police of Nazi Germany.

Ostjuden (Eastern Jew)—Used as insulting term for Yiddish-speaking Jews of Russia and Poland.

Personal effects depot—Where prisoner property was sorted.

POW (Prisoner of War)—They were supposedly protected by the Geneva Convention.

Reichstag—German parliament; had no power after 1933.

RSHA—Combined all police (including Gestapo, SS, SD, and KRIPO). All enemies of the State were sent to concentration camps.

SA—Storm Troopers used by Nazis to fight Communists. Lost influence after 1934.

SD—Security service, the intelligence branch of the SS.

Shtetl—Small Jewish communities in Poland.

Sipo—Secret Police, a branch of the SD.

Sonderkommando—Jewish inmates disposing of bodies in camps. They were usually killed themselves within a month or two.

SS—Guard Corps. Usually identifiable by black uniforms; among other reponsibilities, they ran the concentration camps.

Standing cells—A punishment cell 35 x 35 inches, occupied by four prisoners. After standing all night, they joined work crews during days.

Waffen SS—Military arm of the SS, more loyal to Hitler than the regular army (Wehrmacht).

Wannsee Conference—Meeting in January, 1942, where plans were worked out for the Final Solution.

Wehrmacht—Regular army of Germany.

Zionism—Movement among Jews to establish a Jewish State in Palestine.

ZOB—Jewish Fighting Organization.

Zyklon-B—Hydrogen cyanide crystals used to gas prisoners.

The Roots of Anti-Semitism

Prejudice against Jews did not begin with the Holocaust; it was a long-standing tradition in much of Europe. Pagans seemed more willing to convert to Christianity than the small group of Jews who were present in Europe. The Lateran Councils of 1179 and 1215 put restrictions on all non-Catholics, including Jews. Infidels were required to wear special yellow badges, and they were supposed to live apart from Christians—the beginning of ghettoes. Later, Jews were forced to listen to conversion sermons, and their books were censored and confiscated.

Wild accusations that Jews spread the Black Death and poisoned wells were spread. In one country after another, Jews were driven out. England's King Edward I seized the possessions of the 16,000 Jews living there, and he expelled them from his kingdom. French King Philip the Fair robbed his Jewish subjects and drove them out as well. Germany was not unified, so the Jews driven out of France and England were accepted by the rulers of some German states. Nothing could protect Jews from the prejudice of cruel mobs accusing them of causing a local catastrophe, and many of the Jews were forced to move again, this time to Poland or Italy.

This sixteenth-century Jew was required to wear a badge on his clothing.

Jews in Spain were forced to convert or die. Some, called Marranos, became Catholics. In 1492, all Jews were ordered to leave Spain, and in 1496, they were driven from Portugal. Except for the Marranos and Jews secretly practicing their religion, no Jews remained west of Germany. German and Polish Jews found their only safety was in the confines of the ghetto, and there, they formed a separate society. A few ventured out of the ghetto to become successful in business. Some advised kings on financial matters ("Court Jews"), but most were poor people, marked by a yellow badge and limited in where they could go and what occupations they were allowed to enter. These were the "Dark Ages" for Jews.

Slowly, Jews became more accepted. The Dutch allowed Jews to return during their wars with Spain. In England, after Charles I was beheaded, Oliver Cromwell and the Puritans came to power. The Puritans, strongly anchored in the Old Testament, welcomed Jews back. Roger Williams, founder of Rhode Island, invited Jews to immigrate to his American colony.

In the early nineteenth century, Jews began to become more visible. In one country after another, change was occurring. FRANCE. Napoleon's armies marched across Europe carrying the motto of the French Revolution, "Liberty, Equality, Fraternity," with them. Napoleon called the Jewish leaders together and ordered them to become part of French civilization.

AUSTRIA. The sun seldom shined on Austrian Jews. Queen Maria Theresa hated Jews, and in 1760, she required all unbearded Jews to wear a yellow badge on their left arm. Jews were not allowed to buy vegetables until 9 A.M., or cattle before 11 A.M. Jews were taxed three million florins each year for ten years for the privilege of living in Austria. Joseph II abolished the tax and let Jews attend schools and serve in the army. His successor, Francis II, put Maria Theresa's restrictions back in place. It was not until 1867 that all disabilities were removed; Jews became members of the legislature, and some became generals in the army.

RUSSIA. In the 1790s, Russian armies conquered Poland, and they now had the largest Jewish minority of any nation in the world. The Russians were hard on the Jews; they were denied the right to attend universities or become officers in the army. When anything went wrong in Russia, the Jews were blamed. In 1791, Jews were forced to live in western Russian lands called "The Pale of Settlement." To relieve public unrest in hard times, the government occasionally started a "pogrom," a time when mobs attacked Jews or stole their property without punishment. In 1882, Czar Alexander III took the position that one-third of the Jews should be converted, another one-third should die, and the remaining one-third should be exiled. Many of those exiled came to the United States. Despite all the restrictions put on them, some Russian Jews became successful doctors, engineers, and lawyers. Most, however, were isolated in the small towns *(shtetls)* of what is now Poland, the Ukraine, and western Russia.

HOLLAND. The Jewish community in Holland had a long history, and the synagogue in Amsterdam had been dedicated in 1675. Dutch Jews received full political liberty in 1796. Most lived in Amsterdam, working in the diamond and tobacco industries.

SWEDEN, NORWAY, AND DENMARK were all tolerant of Jews. In Sweden, Jews had all the rights that other non-Lutherans had. Norway and Denmark gave Jews full rights, and a prosperous Jewish community developed in Denmark where they became leaders in banking and business.

GERMANY. Jews in Germany had become so isolated that they could not speak or write in German. Moses Mendellsohn, a brilliant Jewish scholar, overcame that problem by translating the Torah into German. After some important German states gave Jews citizenship, restrictions on Jews were finally lifted in 1870.

Jews were now more visible and could more easily mix and mingle, compete, and excel. The Gentile (non-Jewish) community became aware of them, and they reacted in various ways. To many, the Jew was only slightly different from anyone else, and they had no problem accepting them. Others, called "anti-Semites" saw the Jew as a threat and found excuses to put him in his place. To rally support for their position, anti-Semites brought up medieval accusations against the Jews. They said Jews were Christ-killers, that they drew blood from Gentile children for their passover celebration, and that they plotted against Gentiles. Other anti-Semites looked to new race theories to prove Jews were genetically inferior to Gentiles.

To Jews, freedom from the isolation of the ghetto was a mixed blessing. Now they were exposed to the evil accusations and threats of the outside world.

ACTIVITY:

Hold a discussion in a ghetto between those eager to go out into the Gentile world, and those who are fearful.

Name _____ Date _____

Challenges

1. What did the Lateran Councils force Jews to do? _____

_____

2. What were Marranos? _____

3. What English king drove the Jews out? Who invited them to return? _____

_____

4. What American colony welcomed Jews? _____

5. Why did Napoleon call Jewish leaders in? _____

_____

6. What restrictions did Maria Theresa put on Jews? _____

_____

7. What were pogroms? _____

_____

8. What was the purpose of pogroms? _____

_____

9. How did Mendellsohn teach the German language to Jews? _____

_____

10. What did anti-Semites do to turn public opinion against Jews? _____

_____

Points to Consider

1. Do you think that those who drove Jews from their country might have had some other reasons for their actions rather than just hatred?

2. How would you feel as a Russian Jew if you were being forced to leave Moscow and go to the "Pale of Settlement"?

3. What do the charges made by the anti-Semites against Jews tell about the accusers themselves?

Years of Turmoil in Germany

Wars often begin with a surge of enthusiasm and patriotism, and World War I was no exception. In France, England, Russia, Germany, and Austria, crowds cheered troops as they headed off to war. In Berlin, marching soldiers were handed flowers by admirers on the streets. The Austrian psychiatrist, Sigmund Freud, rejoiced in German victories. Adolf Hitler fell to his knees rejoicing that Heaven had allowed him to live in such a time. He believed war would cleanse Germany of its impurities and build a great future for the German nation.

Behind wars often lie long-standing hatreds. The German Kaiser said: "I hate the Slavs. I know it is a sin, but I can't help hating them." The French wanted revenge on Germany for their 1871 defeat in the Franco-Prussian War. Belgian crowds shouted: "Down with the Germans." Austria's emperor said: "This is war between Teutons and Slavs."

The war soon lost its charm, however, and became a struggle for national survival. The Russians, badly beaten by the Germans, found an easier target, and began driving Jews from small villages in the Pale. Ger-

Germany's president, Paul von Hindenburg, with Adolf Hitler and Hermann Goering in the background

man troops, angered by Belgian resistance, began looting and killing Belgian civilians. POWs held by the Germans were used as manual laborers, digging canals and draining swamps. Some prisoners were forced to stand barefooted in water up to their knees from 6 A.M. to 8 P.M.

The worst cruelty was reserved for the Armenians of Turkey. Conquered in 1515, the Armenians were Christians in a Moslem country, and they had no rights. After Turkey (a German ally) had been beaten back by the Russians, their troops attacked the unarmed Armenians. The 100,000 Armenians in the Turkish army were shot by their officers, and Armenian leaders were arrested and hanged. The Interior Minister sent out an order: "Regardless of women, children, or invalids, and however deplorable the methods of destruction might seem, an end is to be put to their existence." Within seven months of 1915, about 500,000 of the two million Armenians died.

By November 1918, German defeat in the war seemed certain. Mutinies broke out in the army and navy; in cities, Communist-led uprisings occured. On November 10, the Kaiser gave up his throne, and the army informed Chancellor Ebert that it would support the government against a Communist takeover. Germany signed the armistice on November 11.

The TREATY OF VERSAILLES officially ended World War I. German colonies were taken away. Two provinces, Alsace and Lorraine, taken by Germany in 1871, were returned to France. Three treaty provisions especially hurt German pride. (1) The army was reduced to 100,000 men, and it lost its navy and air force. (2) Germany was expected to pay a heavy fine (reparations). (3) Germany was forced to sign the War Guilt clause admitting that the whole war was its fault.

The WEIMAR REPUBLIC replaced Imperial Germany. It got off to a poor start. Violent groups fought for control; leaders were murdered, uprisings *(Putschs)* had to be put down, and ranting politicians and street thugs kept the country in turmoil. Troops returning from the front quietly disappeared as civilians, so the army was of little help in keeping order. A Communist left-wing group, the Sparticists, started a revolt in Berlin. They were attacked by the right-wing *Frei Korps* (Free Corps), and Sparticist leaders were murdered. The *Frei Korps* then went from town to town beating up Communists. In 1920, the government ordered the army to bring the *Frei Korps* under control, but the troops mutinied. The government left Berlin, right-wingers led by Wolfgang Kapp took over the city, but a strike started by left-wingers allowed the government to take over again.

During this time the German economy suffered greatly from the instability and the loss of Alsace and Lorraine. German money dropped in value from 4,500 marks to one U.S. dollar to 4.2 *billion* marks to the dollar. Money was worthless, and desperate Germans turned to the right- or left-wingers for answers. In Saxony, the army crushed a left-wing revolt, and in Bavaria, it stopped the small right-wing Nazi party, and the Nazi leaders were sent to prison.

From 1924 to 1929, Germany's economy made a dramatic comeback. The middle parties (neither right- or left-wing) took control of the *Reichstag* (lower house of the German legislature). Radical groups lost popularity. Suddenly the Great Depression changed all that, however, and in a short time, high unemployment and renewed Communist activity made many middle-class Germans look to Adolf Hitler's Nazis for help.

ADOLF HITLER was born in Austria in 1889. As a boy, Hitler hated anyone who tried to bring him under control, his father and his teachers included. He wrote that in his school days, he met only one Jewish boy and had no opinion on Jews at the time. Hitler dropped out of school in 1915, and went to Vienna where he painted postcards and read anti-Semitic books and racial theories about the natural superiority of Aryans and the animal features of "subhuman" Slavs and Jews.

He served in the German army in World War I, earning two Iron Cross medals for bravery. After he recovered, the army sent him to spy on a small right-wing group called the German Worker's Party—men without a program, leader, or money. He joined as member number 55 and soon be-came member 7 of the executive committee. It was a group to his liking, one he could mold in his image. He changed the name to the NSDAP, usually called Nazis. He made the swastika the party symbol and *"Heil!"* (Hail!) the greeting. He organized a militia, the brown-shirted SA, and formed the SS, his loyal bodyguards. Their "Beer Garden *Putsch*" in 1923 failed, and the leaders were put in prison. While there, Hitler wrote *Mein Kampf* (My Struggle), blaming Jews and Communists for Germany's troubles. No one knew how much suffering would come because of this man and his party.

ACTIVITY:

Make a list of problems faced by the Weimar Republic. If the government of the United States faced these problems, what kind of leader do you think the American people would support?

Name _____ Date _____

Challenges

1. What was the first reaction in Europe to World War I? _____

_____

2. Who did the frustrated Russians attack after they had been beaten by the Germans?

_____

3. Who were the Armenians? What happened to them? _____

_____

4. What did the Treaty of Versailles do to German military power? _____

_____

5. Who had to sign the War Guilt clause, and what did it say? _____

_____

6. Who were the Sparticists, and what happened to them? _____

_____

7. During Germany's inflation, how many marks (German money) did it take to equal $1.

_____

8. What party was Hitler sent to spy on after the war? _____

_____

9. What was the symbol and the greeting developed by Hitler for the NSDAP? _____

_____

10. How could the SA be easily recognized? _____

_____

Points to Consider

1. During World War I, minorities suffered in several countries. How would you account for the cruel treatment they received?
2. Could Hitler have come to power if Germany had been in better financial condition?
3. What kind of person do you think would be drawn to the Nazi party in its early days?

The Nazi Rise to Power

Mein Kampf (My Struggle), Hitler's book, offered a blueprint for Germany's future; few took it seriously in 1923, but by 1939, its effects were being seen, and its author was the center of world attention. Hitler said Germany's crisis had been brought on by outsiders: the French, the "international Jewish conspiracy," and the Communists who were receiving bad advice from Russian Jews. His solution was to wipe out the Jews, destroy the republic, and unite Germans through racial superiority doctrines. He said the duty of government was to protect the *Volk* (the national race) and that could not be done as long as ideas of equality and majority rule continued. The *Volk* needed a leader, a *Führer,* to guide them. The people were to blindly follow because only he understood what was good for them.

Adolf Hitler

When prosperity returned to Germany in the mid-1920s, the Germans turned away from the radicals, and the Nazi party was shrinking. Inside the party, Gregor Strasser battled Hitler for the leader's role, but lost. As Hitler looked at the failure of the Beer Garden *Putsch,* he realized that the way to gain power was through politics, not revolution. When the German economy failed in 1929, he realized his time had come. Hitler allied the Nazis with the Nationalist party, which was closer to the business leaders, financial support, and respectability. In 1928, only 12 Nazis were in the *Reichstag* (the lower house of the German legislature); the 1930 election gave them 107 seats. *Reichstag* sessions were interrupted by unruly Nazi members, and street battles were common between the SA and Communists.

Affairs were so unsettled that three elections were held in 1932 for seats in the *Reichstag.* In those elections, Nazis got 33, 37, and 32 percent of the seats. If Communists and Socialists had united, they could have ruled. However, Chancellor Von Papen, a moderate, offered a deal to the Nazis. Hitler would become chancellor, Von Papen would become vice-chancellor, and Von Papen's friends were to have important jobs. On January 30, 1933, President Hindenburg reluctantly accepted the arrangement and appointed Hitler as chancellor. It was a tragic mistake.

Hitler called for new elections in March and used every trick to win. A fire at the *Reichstag* was blamed on a Dutch Communist. Opposition parties were denied radio time, their political rallies were broken up, and Nazi thugs threatened voters on their way to the polls. Hitler received 43 percent of the vote. He would not have had a majority in the *Reichstag,* but Communists who had been elected were not allowed to take their seats.

THE NAZI RULERS. Everyone in the German government became the obedient servant of the *Führer;* as long as they worshiped him, they were free to commit any crimes they wanted as long as it was not too embarrassing. Goering stole valuable art for his private collection. Goebbels had love affairs. Himmler became wealthy by renting out concentration camp inmates to be slave laborers for big companies. Heydrich was a cruel man who enjoyed watching others suffer, and Roehm enjoyed food and drink almost as much as torturing and killing a Jew or Communist. All of these people were part of the story of war, brutality, and murder that followed.

HERMAN GOERING had been a pilot during World War I and had received the highest military honor, the Pour lë Merite for heroism. After the war, he became a commercial pilot. Joining the Nazis in 1922, he was wounded in the "Beer Garden *Putsch*," but escaped arrest. Pain from his wounds caused him to become a morphine addict. In 1932, he became president of the *Reichstag*. He often held several high positions at the same time. As the Prussian minister of the interior, he organized political police (the Gestapo); in 1934, he gave that job to Himmler. Goering had qualities most Nazi leaders lacked; he was polite, interested in culture, and had a jolly appearance. As good natured as he looked, however he was a ruthless, greedy man.

JOSEPH GOEBBELS was a little man with a bad limp, which had prevented him from serving in World War I. He also had a Ph.D. degree and insisted on being called "Dr. Goebbels." His job was Minister of Propaganda, and he boasted: "Propaganda made the Third Reich." It was said of him: "He lies in everything and admires himself for it, and he mocks the masses who fall for him." To stir up opinion, he repeated the same lie over and over. He accused Jews of being at the heart of Germany's problem, and said they deserved anything that was done to them. All German newspapers became "racially clean" after the Reich Press Law was passed in October 1933. No journalist could be Jewish or married to a Jew. Jewish publications were shut down. Newspapers could only tell the public what the Nazis wanted told.

HEINRICH HIMMLER was a chicken farmer who joined the Nazi party in 1925, became one of the elite SS in 1927, and within two years, was its leader. When he took over, the SS only had 280 members and was a branch of the SA. By 1933, the SS had 50,000 members and had begun "security checks" on all Nazis, except Hitler. In appearance, there was nothing unusual about Himmler, but his talent for organization and his secret files made him the second most powerful leader in Germany.

Himmler was devoted to creating the Master Race and destroying the inferior races. He said: "Nature is cruel; therefore, we may be cruel, too." Himmler divided the police into the Ordo (regular police) and Sipo (secret police). The Sipo were divided into Gestapo (political police) and Kripo (criminal police). The Gestapo was feared by everyone: Jews, political opponents, or anyone daring to complain about Nazi rule. All of these men were ambitious, clever, and never to be trusted.

REINHARD HEYDRICH, Himmler's choice to lead the Gestapo, and ERNST ROEHM, head of the SA were men without consciences. Heydrich worked more behind the scenes, but Roehm was more noticeable. His SA had been useful in putting Hitler in power, but when their street brawling was no longer needed, Roehm and other SA leaders were shot in June 1934.

ACTIVITY:

Pretend that you live in Nazi Germany and have absolute control over every word in the newspaper. Take a copy of your local newspaper and censor every article that criticizes the president, the police, and the courts or praises any group opposing what they are doing.

Name _____ Date _____

Challenges

1. Who did Hitler blame Germany's problems on in *Mein Kampf?* _____

_____

2. Who are the *Volk,* and what official did Hitler say should make their decisions for them?

_____

3. Why did Hitler join the Nazi party to the Nationalist party? _____

_____

4. What parties could have ruled in Germany in 1932 if they had worked together? _____

_____

5. Who helped Hitler become German chancellor? What did he expect to get in return?

_____

_____

6. What did Goering do that might have caused him to be arrested in any other country?

_____

7. What did Himmler do that made him rich? _____

_____

8. Who was the Minister of Propaganda? How did he get his points across? _____

_____

9. What was the job of the Gestapo? _____

_____

10. What happened to Roehm? _____

_____

Points to Consider

1. How do you think most Americans would react if men in brown shirts threatened them on their way to vote?

2. Why is it dangerous for any government official like Himmler to be able to gather personal information on anyone?

3. Roehm had been close to Hitler from the beginning, but when the SS came to arrest him, the only choice he had was whether to kill himself or let the SS do it for him. What does this say about Hitler?

The Nazi View of Religion and Race

The first of the Ten Commandments is: "You shall have no other gods before me." Jesus told his followers not to fear those who can only kill the body, but to fear God who has the power to cast into hell. Religion threatens the dictator because it says there is a higher Authority than the ruler. The Nazis knew they could not remove religion, but then tried to twist it to conform to their purposes. Hitler had only contempt for religion and its concern over ethics, mercy, and God's judgment.

Hitler saw himself as the "messiah," of a German god who said: "Let iron grow," and armed his Aryan chosen people with the "saber, sword, and spear." Hitler's god backed Germany in anything it did to create a world free of racial poisoning by Jews and other "subhuman" races. The image of Hitler given

Dr. Martin Niemöller was the leader of the Confessional church in Ger-

by the German press was that of perfection. His habits were pure: no drinking, smoking or even eating meat. He was too devoted to Germany to need a woman's companionship (the public knew nothing of his girlfriend, Eva Braun). He never admitted to a mistake, and none of his "disciples" criticized him in public. He was the chosen one who would free Germany from its enemies: the foreigners, Communists, Jews, and other "subhumans." He was too modest to claim perfection, but he let others do it for him.

At first, many Christians supported him because they feared the atheistic Communists. By 1937, however, many realized how dangerous he was.

CATHOLICS. When he came to power, Hitler signed the Concordat of 1933 with the Catholic church. He agreed to protect the church, its property, and cultural societies. In return, the church would stay out of German politics. It was not long before youth groups were broken up, monks were falsely accused of smuggling gold out of Germany, and priests were accused of immoral behavior. Pope Pius XI ordered that a letter, "With Burning Anxiety," be read from the pulpit of every German church. In it, he accused Hitler of breaking his agreement with the church.

The Archbishop of Bavaria, Cardinal Faulhaber dared to call the Jews "God's chosen people" and warned Catholics against race prejudice. Nazi mobs attacked his home, but he would not back down.

PROTESTANTS. Hitler called Protestants "insignificant little people, submissive as dogs." When he appointed a Nazi to be bishop, ministers refused to accept his authority. Dr. Martin Niemöller, a World War I naval hero, was now minister of a large church outside Berlin. At first, he supported Hitler because he feared the Communists, but he refused to let Hitler rule his conscience. He became leader of the Confessional (traditional Lutheran) church, and about 6,000 ministers joined his movement. Within a short time, many were sent to concentration camps. Niemöller was not so easy to handle, but in 1937, he was sent to Dachau.

The GERMAN FAITH MOVEMENT was Hitler's distortion of Christianity. Its doctrines were: (1) Jesus was Aryan, not Jewish; (2) The Old Testament had no place in Germany; and (3) German land and blood were the sacred elements. Traditional Christian morality was thrown out by the Nazis. It was less important that a child have married parents than that it be Aryan. If Hitler had won the war, he intended to eliminate Christianity from Europe.

Race. A popular idea of the 1930s was eugenics; its main goal was to produce the genetically perfect child. This belief stated that if Race A is the best, mixing with Race B or C could only produce an inferior offspring. Almost every society believes it is better than others; we call this "chauvinism" (sho-ve-nism). At the time of the French Revolution, Count de Gobineau divided races into white, yellow, and black. Whites were the best, and the best whites were "Aryans." He warned that too much mixing weakened the superior Aryan race. An English writer, Houston Chamberlain, went further, claiming that Nordics (the cream of Aryans) were by right, masters of the world. He said Jews were a disruptive force in history.

Nazis taught that Aryans were the super race and had superior intelligence and beauty. They had blond hair, blue eyes, and fair skin. The fact that there never was an Aryan race (Aryan was a language group, not a people) never bothered the Nazis. Within this non-existent Aryan race were the Nordic Teutons (German) who were considered the best, followed by Anglo-Saxons (English), and Celts (French).

Richard Wagner, the opera composer, added to the racial myth. He hated Jews: "The Jew speaks the language of the nation…but he always speaks as an alien."Wagner glorified Germany's pagan past, a time before the "subhumans" arrived, when German blood was pure. Hitler was a great fan of Wagner and attended a Wagner festival each year. He sat for hours dreaming of what Germany might be if it didn't have Jews within its borders.

Besides ridding Germany of inferior races, two other changes were needed to protect Aryan blood. One was to stop genetic inferiors from producing more of their kind. Mental and physical weaklings were to be eliminated. A Nazi doctor said: "The solution of the problem of the mentally ill becomes easy if one eliminates these people." In time, programs were developed to shorten the lives of those who weakened the master race.

The second change was to stress physical fitness so that boys might become strong soldiers and girls could produce healthy sons. Developing thinking skills was the least important job of education for boys and girls.

When war began, Himmler feared that too many Aryans would be killed. He started a program called *Lebensborn* (Fountain of Life) to encourage women to produce Aryan children, and when World War II began, he sent squads into Poland to kidnap Polish children with Aryan qualities. In religion and race, the Nazis had no moral scruples.

ACTIVITY:

If there were a "Master Race," what qualities would that race have in today's world? You might list physical and mental qualities and skills. What important people in your life or in the world *do not* have those qualities?

Name _____ Date _____

Challenges

1. Why didn't Hitler like Jesus' teachings about who should be feared? _____

_____

2. What did Hitler see as his god-given mission? _____

_____

3. What did the Catholic church promise in the Concordat of 1933? _____

_____

4. What did Pope Pius XI accuse Hitler of doing? _____

_____

5. Who was the leader of the Confessional church? What did Hitler do to him? _____

_____

6. What did the German Faith Movement say about Jesus' birth? _____

_____

7. What is eugenics? _____

_____

8. What did Hitler think could be done to stop handicapped children from being born? _____

_____

9. What was the least important goal of education in Nazi Germany? _____

_____

10. How did Himmler try to make up for the loss of Aryans during the war? _____

_____

Points to Consider

1. Why was it important to the Nazis to portray Hitler as perfect?
2. What risks did church leaders face when they stood up to the Nazis?
3. Why do you think Hitler did not put more stress on developing mental ability in the children of his Master Race.

The Nazi Attack on German Jews Begins

The Nazis made no secret of their beliefs from the beginning. (1) Germany had lost World War I because Jews and Communists undermined morale. (2) They were racists who believed inferior races threatened the *Volk's* blood line. (3) Jews were not German; they were only "guests." (4) The feeble-minded and deformed must be prevented from producing more of their kind. (5) Traditional religious teachings about duty to God and brotherhood weakened the nation. (6) They were anxious to put their beliefs into law. No judge could help an accused "enemy of the State" escape.

DEFINING WHO WAS JEWISH. Who were the Jews? School children were taught they had noses shaped like the number "6." A reader of the Nazi newspaper, *Der Sturmer,* learned they were repulsive, fat men who tried to lure Aryan children into their cars. Hitler described them as rich bankers, traitors, and trade union leaders. By those definitions, all the Jews would have fit into a small prison. In fact, Jews dressed, looked, and acted like any other German. That similarity created a problem for the Nazis in deciding who was Jewish.

In Vienna, Austria, Jews were forced to display the word *Jude* on their stores after the Anschluss.

Separating Jews from Gentiles was confusing because many had married Gentiles or had converted to Christianity. How far back did a German have to trace his ancestry to prove he was Aryan? In the early days, Nazis were not sure how to solve these questions. They finally worked out a complicated formula in the Nuremberg Laws of 1935. *Jews and Mischlenges* (mongrels or mixed bloods) were those who had practiced Judaism, had Jewish grandparents, or were married to Jews. There were so many sub-categories that few understood exactly where the law placed them.

RESTRICTIONS BEGIN. Even before there was a definition, Hitler ordered that all non-Aryan government officials be retired. "Non-Aryan" was then defined as anyone with a parent or grandparent who practiced Judaism. All newspaper workers who were Jewish were fired; then Goebbels expelled Jews from the guilds of musicians, writers, and artists. Without guild mem-bership, a person could not perform or display his or her works. Businesses were pressured to fire Jewish executives. Companies and banks owned by Jews were hit by SA-sponsored boycotts. In case the customer did not know that the store where he shopped was Jewish-owned, SA or SS "defensive guards" stood outside to inform them. At first, these boycotts did not work because the public needed the services the store or professional man supplied.

To separate Jews from Aryan school children, a law was issued in April 1933, "The Law Against Overcrowding of German Schools." At first, it only limited the number of Jews in universities, but by 1938, Jewish children were not permitted to attend schools. By then, Jews were no longer allowed to use swimming pools. A Jew was never certain what new restriction was going to be imposed on him or her.

The Nuremberg Laws of September 1935 said Jews were not German citizens (they were "subjects"). Jews could not marry Aryans and could not employ Aryan women under 35 years old. The Reich Citizenship Law was passed in November 1935, and took away the right of Jews to vote or hold public office.

After that, pressure let up on Jews. The 1936 Olympics were to be held in Berlin, and Hitler did not want the foreign press writing vicious truths about his Jewish policy. During the games, the only indication of Nazi hatred for "subhumans" was Hitler's snubbing of black athletes. After the foreign guests were gone, gangs of young bullies returned to beating up helpless Jews. The Jews became careful about where they went, and when.

AUSTRIA. Hitler had long spoken of *Lebensraum* (living room) for the new Germany, and Austria was an obvious place to expand. He sent Nazis into Austria to create enthusiasm for the union *(Anschluss)* of the two countries. A vote was taken in Austria, and 90 percent favored uniting with Germany. For Austria's large Jewish population, this was tragic. Anti-Semitism ran strong in Austria, and to show their support for Hitler, Austrians outdid the Germans in persecuting Jews. Jews were dragged from their homes and shops and forced to clean latrines, sidewalks, and grafitti on the walls of buildings. While the Jews worked, their homes were looted. A concentration camp was established at Mauthausen, and Austrian Jewish prisoners were sent there to work in the quarry. Many Jews were willing to give up everything they owned for the privilege of leaving Austria.

KRISTALLNACHT. In 1938, a German-born Jew of Polish-Russian ancestry in Paris was outraged by news that his family was being deported to Poland. Seeking revenge, he killed Ernst vom Rath, a minor official at the German embassy in Paris. Secretly delighted, Goebbels pretended to be outraged and unleashed his thugs to attack Jews.

November 9, 1938, became known as *Kristallnacht* (Night of the Broken Glass). Jewish property was destroyed or damaged all over Germany, and over 90 Jews were killed. Police were ordered not to interfere as mobs smashed, looted, and burned stores, synagogues, and homes. The looters, though dressed as civilians, wore the heavy boots of uniformed Nazi party members. The New York *Times* estimated total damage at $400 million. Because this was the result of German "righteous indignation," the Jews had to pay one billion marks (about $400 million) as punishment for Rath's murder. Insurance claims by Jews were seized by the government. In January 1939, all Jewish shops were to be closed.

In 1933, there were about 700,000 Jews in Germany and Austria. In 1938 and 1939, 403,000 left. Few left behind wanted to stay, but it was very difficult to find a country willing to take them. In 1940, the U.S. embassy in Berlin had 248,000 immigration applications on file; the U.S. quota allowed only 27,000 Germans a year into the country.

ACTIVITY:

Your classroom has become a meeting place for Jews. It is November 8, 1938, and those present are discussing whether to leave Germany or stay. Appoint a student to argue for going and another to argue for staying.

Name _____ Date _____

Challenges

1. The Nazis said Jews were not citizens. What was their new status after 1935? _____
_____

2. *Mischlenge* was the term used for those with some Jewish blood. What did the term mean in

English? _____

3. During the boycotts of Jewish merchants, who would greet you at the door to tell you this busi-

ness was owned by Jews?   _____

4. How did the Reich Citizenship Law affect Jews? _____
_____

5. Why did pressure ease on German Jews for a while in 1936? _____
_____

6. How did Austrians feel about uniting with Germany? _____
_____

7. What concentration camp was established for Austrian Jews? _____
_____

8. What was the excuse for *Kristallnacht?* _____
_____

9. What does *Kristallnacht* mean in English? _____
_____

10. How many Jews left Germany and Austria in 1938 and 1939? How many refugees would the

U.S. accept in a year? _____

Points to Consider

1. One thing the Nazis tried to do was make Jews seem less than human. How did the term "Mischlenge" do that?

2. If you were a young Jew in Berlin, how might the possibility of meeting some Nazi thugs on the street affect the way you did things?

3. Austrians are ordinarily very nice people. What reasons might explain their behavior after the *Anschluss?*

The Drive to the East
(Drang nach Osten)

Hitler saw himself as the son of destiny, and never made a secret of his desire to expand Germany to include all areas where a German minority lived. Austrians, except for the Jewish minority, were good Aryans who spoke German. To bring them into Germany was easy. To the east, there were large German minorities in Czechoslovakia, Poland, and Russia, oppressed minorities ruled by inferior races.

CZECHOSLOVAKIA. As soon as Czech Jews learned of the *Anschluss,* they began selling off their property. A large, Jewish-

A German soldier escorts Polish prisoners after the invasion of Poland, which officially started World War II.

controlled bank sold out at a bargain price to the German Dresdner Bank in February 1938. After England and France agreed to let Germany have the Sudeten region of Czechoslovakia at the Munich Conference, Nazi troops moved into the region. The Czechs were defenseless, and Jews crowded into the Prague railroad station and airport, ready to buy a ticket to go anywhere to escape. On March 15, 1938, German troops marched into Czechoslovakia. Hitler was delighted with his easy victory, but it came with a catch. He had 356,000 new Jews. There were now more Jews in Nazi-held territory than when he came to power.

POLAND. Jews had a long history in Poland where King Casimir had invited Jews driven out of other nations to come to his country in 1364. Polish Jews had been protected during the Inquisition, when thousands of Jews were being killed in other lands. Eastern Poland, in the region called Kresy, had a Jewish majority. There, Jewish market towns called *shtetls* (pronounced shtey-tels) developed; these had a central market square surrounded by workshops, stores, and houses. A few Christians lived in the *shtetls,* and most worked for Jews. Kresy's Jews spoke Yiddish (a German dialect mixed with Hebrew, Aramaic, and Slavic words), not Polish.

While Poland ruled, Kresy lived under Jewish law interpreted by Jewish judges. After Russia conquered the region in the 1700s, Empress Catherine I ordered that Ukrainian Jews be deported beyond the frontier, and they were not to enter Russia again under any circumstance. Now Jews were forced to live under Russian law as interpreted by Russian judges.

While Jews were the majority in the Kresy region, they were a distinct minority in Polish cities. Despite prejudice against them, the Jewish population in Warsaw reached 300,000 by 1939. In Krakow, the story was similar; at times anti-Jewish feeling ran strong, but large Jewish communities developed.

In the 1930s, anti-Semitism grew in Poland. Many Jews lived in deep poverty, nearly half earning less than ten dollars a week. Drought hit the Kresy, and many Jews there were starving. Even German Jews looked down on Polish Jews with their caftans and sidelocks, and used *"Ostjuden"* (Eastern Jew) as an insulting term. Many Poles disliked the successful Jews. Over one-third of all doctors, over half of all lawyers, and nearly one-fourth of university students were Jews. This caused jealousy and tension even before the Nazis came. The Polish Nara party was racist like the Nazis, and from 1937 to 1939, began making Jews miserable.

In 1938, Germany rounded up thousands of Jews of Polish descent in the middle of the night, hustled them to railroad stations without luggage, clothing, or food, and shipped them in sealed trains to the Polish border. The Poles refused to let them enter, and they countered by sending a train loaded with Polish Jews of German descent to the border. A deal was worked out. Poland accepted 7,000 Polish Jews, the Germans accepted a few German Jews, and all the rest were left to walk home.

The fall of Czechoslovakia left Poland surrounded on three sides by the jaws of the German tiger. Their only hope was that Russia would protect them. They did not know that Hitler and Stalin had worked out a deal to divide Poland between them. England and France warned Germany that an attack on Poland would force them to declare war on Germany. On September 1, 1939, Germany attacked Poland, and on September 3, England and France declared war. After German troops entered Poland, Russia moved into eastern Poland. Terrible times faced Poland's 31 million Gentiles and 3 million Jews.

RUSSIAN-HELD POLAND. The Communists were no friends of Jews. They closed Jewish schools and seized hospital equipment, power plants, and private property. The NKVD (secret police) shipped Jews to forced labor camps and used former prison inmates as police. Desperate Jews begged to enter German-held Poland. A German officer asked them: "Jews, where are you going? Don't you see that we are going to kill you?"

The Russians and Germans agreed to prevent opposition by killing all Poles who might lead uprisings, whether they were Jews or Gentiles. Polish army officers in Russian hands were executed by the NKVD. In Russian-held Poland, two million Poles (about 30 percent Jewish) were sent to work in labor camps or were drafted into the Red Army. By October 1942, 900,000 of those were dead.

GERMAN-HELD POLAND. As head of the SD, Reinhard Heydrich began the process of controlling and eliminating Polish Jews and any Gentiles who dared to help them. He had no concern for human life, but was very clever. He removed Jews from *shtetls* and the Gentile sections of cities and sent them to ghettos. In the ghetto, he set up a Jewish council *(Judenrat)* to give the appearance that the suffering of Jews was caused by their own leaders. Jews were required to wear a Star of David on armbands. Those between 14 and 60 years of age were required to work on slave labor projects. In 1941, the food allowance in Warsaw was 2,613 calories for Germans, 669 calories for Poles, and 184 calories for Jews.

Heydrich convinced many Jews that their troubles were caused by the Poles, not the Germans. As proof, he arranged for Jewish laborers to be pelted with rocks by Germans dressed as Polish civilians. At the same time, he warned Poles to stay away from the ghettos. Any Pole caught smuggling food into the ghetto or hiding a Jew was shot.

ACTIVITY:

Looking at bread wrappers and labels on cans, how much might a person eat or drink to reach the 184 calories allowed for Warsaw Jews?

Name _____ Date _____

Challenges

1. What were *shtetls?* _____

2. What was Kresy? _____

_____

3. What was the attitude of German Jews toward Polish Jews? _____

_____

4. What was the Polish equivalent of the Nazi party? _____

5. What did the Russians do to Polish Jews? _____

_____

6. Why did Jews try to enter German-held Poland? _____

_____

7. Why did England and France declare war on Germany? _____

_____

8. What were the *Judenrat?* _____

_____

9. How did Heydrich trick Jews into believing the Polish Gentiles were causing their misery?

_____

10. What was the Warsaw food allowance for Germans, Poles, and Jews? _____

_____

Points to Consider

1. What clues from the recent past let Czech Jews know how serious their situation was when the Sudeten was lost?

2. Many Polish Jews spoke only Yiddish. What effect do you think that may have had on their relations with Christian Poles?

3. What kind of Poland do you think the Russians and Germans were trying to create? How were they trying to reach that goal?

Hitler Attacks Western Europe

At first, the English and French declaration of war against Germany in September 1939 seemed to be an empty threat. While the Nazis were invading Poland with their dramatic *blitzkrieg* (lightning war), the Western powers were accused of waging "sitzkrieg" and "phony war." Western nations hoped Hitler's appetite for conquest would be satisfied by eastward expansion.

That illusion ended abruptly in April and May 1940, with quick German victories over Denmark, Norway, Belgium, the Netherlands, and Luxembourg. The invasion of France began in May; by June, France surrendered. Germany occupied northern France, but a puppet Vichy government under Marshal Philippe Petain was created to rule southern France. The Jewish population of the conquered nations included 8,000 Danes, 1,900 Norwegians, 90,000 Belgians, 140,000 Dutch, 4,500 Luxembourgers, and 175,000 French (not including 175,000 German refugees who had fled to France earlier).

Hitler poses in front of the Eiffel Tower during a brief visit to occupied Paris on June 23, 1940.

DENMARK. Unlike other nations, Denmark was seized without bloodshed and was "racially pure" (as Aryan as Germany). King Christian X and the legislature stayed in Denmark. At first, Germany treated it differently than other conquered nations. The Danes had no prejudice against Jews. The Germans told the king to solve his "Jewish problem." He answered that there was no Jewish problem: "We know we are their equals."

BELGIUM. Belgium's Jews were located mostly in Antwerp (50,000) and Brussels (30,000). After Hitler came to power, 30,000 German Jews moved to Belgium. On one occasion, desperate German Jews sent a train filled with children to Belgium to be cared for by the Jewish community.

Belgium was unable to put up much resistance when the Germans invaded, so Jews had no time to escape. The pro-German Rexists helped carry out anti-Jewish policies, but many others in Belgium had no desire to help find and abuse Jews. Other problems for the Germans included (1) the lack of wealth possessed by Belgian Jews, (2) the lack of SS manpower to carry out Hitler's policies, (3) military concerns were a higher priority than racial policy, and (4) Belgian interference.

German officials complained that Belgians did not "understand the Jewish question." After the Star of David was required, teachers explained it was a mark of distinction for Jewish children. Banks were very slow to send records of Jewish depositors to the authorities. After Nazis refused to give ration cards to Jewish children, the Belgian Red Cross fed them. Many Jews refused to wear the Star of David and failed to show up for labor details. Gentile families took children in, and false identity cards were forged for them. When German occupation ended in 1944, about 65,000 Belgian Jews had escaped the concentration and death camps.

NETHERLANDS. Dutch Jews faced two serious problems: (1) Their nation was small with no place to hide, and (2) the Germans sent officials there who were enthused about removing Jews. Reich Commissar Arthur Seyss-Inquart was an Austrian Nazi fanatic who told the Dutch: "The Jews for us are not Dutchmen. They are enemies with whom we can come neither to an armistice or a peace."

As in other countries, the Nazis seized Jewish property. In January 1941, Jews and Mischlenges were required to register. Dutch Nazis began attacking the Jewish neighborhoods in Amsterdam. The Germans demanded the Jews set up a council to control the Jewish section of Amsterdam. After the Germans deported 400 young Jews to the Mauthausen concentration camp, shipyard workers started a general strike. The SS blamed it on the Jews and said unless it ended, they would suffer. In April 1942, Jews were required to wear the Star of David.

At Mauthausen, the Dutch prisoners were forced to carry heavy rocks up a steep slope. After a time, many joined hands and jumped to their deaths.

Hans Rauter, SS commander for Holland, was determined to capture every Jew in the country. Any Aryan helping Jews hide or escape was sent to a concentration camp. By the time German occupation ended in 1944, three out of four Dutch Jews had been killed, and their seized property had been taken to Germany.

FRANCE. The Jewish population of France had doubled after the Nazis came to power. Besides French citizens, there were German, Belgian, and Dutch Jewish refugees. Many in France sympathized with the Jews, but others strongly supported Nazi racial policy. There were Nazi newspapers like *Au Pilori* and anti-Semites like writer Louis-Ferdinand Céline, who could not understand why the army was not bayoneting Jews.

In June 1940, all Jews in France were required to wear the yellow star. Petain issued "certificates of Aryanization" to some Jews, exempting them from wearing the badge. Those Jews not exempted and caught without a badge risked being reported by informers. The first roundup of foreign Jews in occupied France was planned for July 7, 1942; 888 police units and 400 young Fascists joined in the raids. Captured Jews were taken in buses to an indoor sports arena.

Parents were separated from children and taken in cattle trucks to Drancy, and from there, to death camps. Then came the job of removing 4,000 children, all under 12 years of age. French gendarmes (police) were told to put the children on cattle cars. A line of scared, crying children moved to the railroad yard. One boy reached out of a car to a Red Cross lady, and an officer struck his hand hard. A German writer said of that incident: "Not for a single moment can I forget how I am surrounded by wretched people…in torment." None of the children survived the war.

The Nazi goal of a *Judenfrei* Europe was more successful in some of occupied Western Europe than in other parts. Anyone who was Jewish could not rest peacefully for many days to come.

ACTIVITY:

Act out a discussion in a Jewish family that has just been ordered to wear the yellow Star of David. Someone in the family thinks they should not, and someone else thinks they should. Have the class discuss their dilemma. Remind the class they do not know yet what is ahead for them.

Name _____ Date _____

Challenges

1. What nicknames were given to the English and French war on Germany (1939–40)?

_____

2. Which nation in Western Europe had the most native-born Jews? _____

3. Why did the Nazis treat Denmark better than other countries at first? _____

_____

4. How did the attitude of Belgian bankers help Jews? _____

_____

5. How many Belgian Jews were killed during the Holocaust? _____

6. What did Dutch Jews do to end their misery at Mauthausen? _____

_____

7. Who were two Nazi officials in Holland who wanted to kill Jews? _____

_____

8. What did Céline think the army should be doing? _____

_____

9. How did Petain protect some Jews, at least for a while? _____

_____

10. How young were the children whose parents were taken away in the first roundup?

_____

Points to Consider

1. What was the point of King Christian X's remark? What would have been the Nazi reaction to it?

2. Why was it important to the Nazis that Jews in all these countries be required to wear a Star of David?

3. Try to think of words that would describe the feelings of the French Jewish children when their parents were taken away.

The Germans Invade Russia

Hitler's successes in the East caused him to risk more daring schemes that had never worked before: bombing England into surrender and invading Russia. Neither would succeed; instead, they led to the downfall of the Nazi government.

Stalin and Hitler had many things in common. Both had alcoholic fathers, were radicals at a young age, and were very ambitious. Both took advantage of opportunities that came their way to rise to the top, and both were willing to sacrifice even their longtime friends and associates to stay there. Just as Hitler killed the leaders of the SA, Stalin began a purge in Russia

Germans try to move an anti-tank gun through Soviet territory being burned according to Josef Stalin's "scorched earth" policy.

that lasted from 1934 to 1939. Even the highest officials had to watch everyone; no one could be trusted. Altogether, Stalin was probably responsible for even more deaths than Hitler. Stalin observed that the death of one person was a tragedy, but the death of a million was a statistic.

Despite a treaty with Stalin, Hitler planned to attack the Soviet Union. He was aware that Russia had millions of Jews, a challenge to his goal of all German-held territory being cleansed of Jews. He also knew many Ukrainians and Russians hated Jews. As plans were made for the invasion, the Jewish question was one of the big considerations. The task of wiping out so many people required creating a new unit, the *Einsatzgruppen* (mobile killing squads). These were to follow the army and kill any Jews they found. With so many Jews in western Russia, they would have no trouble finding victims. Russia's Jews were easy targets. They often lived in small, isolated villages, had been treated badly by the Russians, and knew so little about the Germans that they greeted them as liberators.

The Germans caught the Russians by surprise and moved eastward with little opposition. At first, the *Einsatzgruppen* killed 100,000 Jews a month, but when the figures dropped, they searched for those they had missed. By that time, most Jews had died or escaped from the region.

GERMAN SUCCESS. Moving into western Ukraine, the Germans were treated like heroes by the people. For example, at Rovno, a city about 100 miles east of the Polish border, there were many Jewish refugees. When the invasion began in June 1941, many Jewish men joined the retreating Red Army, and others who could travel joined the refugees; the elderly and women with young children stayed. After the Germans arrived, Rovno's police killed 1,300 Jews on the streets. A *Judenrat* was established, and following German orders, it told Jews to assemble at the central square. They were to bring no more than 35 pounds of personal belongings.

They were taken into the woods to deep trenches dug by Russian POWs. Despite the bitter cold, they were ordered to take off all their clothes. They were led to the edge of the trench, and forced to jump. About 17,500 Jews died on November 6 and 7. Others were not sent to the trench, but the only way for them to get food was to work for the Germans. One job was sorting the belongings of those who had died. To live, one had to help the murderer.

At Viteps, in White Russia, most Jews died of starvation before the Germans moved the ghetto from one side of the river to the other. Even then, they would not let the Jews use the bridge. Many drowned while trying to wade across, and those using boats or rafts were machine-gunned.

GERMAN PROBLEMS. The murder of helpless people was not as easy as it looked. (1) Little effort was made at first to keep onlookers away, and some took pictures or wrote letters home about the slaughter. These pictures and accounts made the war seem less glorious, and it was feared there might be a public outcry against it. (2) Killing people caused even hardened soldiers to become disgusted with the process, and they started suffering nightmares, alcoholism, and health problems. (3) It was simply murder, and that would not look good on paper.

To solve these problems, they began using Romanians and Ukrainians to do their dirty work. To make their actions seem almost noble, they used phrases like "resettlement," "executive measure," "cleaning up of the Jewish question," "major cleaning actions," and lastly, "final solution."

No phrase could hide what was going on from the executioners. When Himmler watched 100 prisoners being shot, he was shaken. He spoke to the troops, explaining their task was a "repulsive duty," but they were only obeying orders. He alone had to stand before God and Hitler to explain their actions. After that experience, Himmler began looking for a better way to kill Jews and dispose of bodies.

RUSSIANS AND RUMANIANS. Many in the Baltic countries (Latvia, Lithuania, and Estonia) taken by Russia in 1940 did not like Jews or Russians. When the Germans marched in, they were greeted as heroes by the people. It was not only fear of angering the Germans, but enthusiasm for getting rid of Jews that caused Gentiles to turn their backs on Jews begging for food and shelter. In Lithuania, the people were eager to burn synagogues and kill Jews. At Kovno, 1,500 Jews were killed by mobs in two nights.

The Rumanian allies of Germany carried out their own persecution of Jews. Rumanians had treated Jews badly since the 19th century, and pogroms of killing, looting, and persecuting had been common. A group called the Iron Guard persuaded Rumanians that the nation's weak economy could be improved by seizing Jewish property.

During the war, many Rumanians volunteered for *Einsatzgruppe D,* which impressed even the Germans with their enthusiasm for killing Jews.

After a 1941 Russian air raid on Iasi (pronounced Jassy), Jews were falsely accused of signaling the attackers. Thousands of Jews were put in boxcars and left to starve. Others were sent to concentration and death camps. Fortunately, a Jewish lawyer named Wilhelm Filderman was a friend of the Rumanian dictator, and he convinced him not to send more. About 300,000 Rumanian Jews survived.

ACTIVITY:

You work in Goebbel's Propaganda Ministry. Reports of the deaths at Rovno have been heard by reporters from neutral nations, and they want an explanation of what happened. How would you explain it?

Name _____ Date _____

Challenges

1. What did Stalin do in Russia that was similar to Hitler's murder of the SA? _____
_____

2. What was the purpose of *Einsatzgruppen*? _____
_____

3. What happened to the number of Jews found on the second sweep by the mobile squads?
_____

4. What Jews had remained behind at Rovno? _____
_____

5. How were Jews at Rovno killed? _____
_____

6. Where did Jews at Viteps die? _____
_____

7. How did their jobs affect the lives of those assigned to mobile squads? _____
_____

8. What phrase did Himmler use to describe their job? _____

9. How did Lithuanians show their hatred of Jews? _____
_____

10. What happened to the Jews at Iasi who were put in boxcars? _____
_____

Points to Consider

1. What made it so easy for the mobile squads to kill so many Jews at first? Do you think it could be done as easily now? Why?
2. Why did the Nazis prefer phrases like "resettlement" and "major cleaning action" to the truth?
3. What motives, other than anti-Semitism, might explain what happened to Jews in Russia and Rumania?

Establishing Concentration Camps

Every nation punishes those who have murdered, robbed, or violated the law in some other way. In early times, execution by cruel means, torture, slavery, seizing of property, or punishing the family as well as the lawbreaker were common. In modern times, the usual punishments are fines, terms in prison, or execution. Torture was discarded

Prisoners might be forced to stand for hours during roll call in German concentration camps.

in most Western nations by the time of the French Revolution. The numbers of prisoners at any given time were small enough that they could be dealt with in an orderly way. In contrast, Hitler's concentration camps were (1) deliberately brutal, (2) determined to work people to death, and (3) were to exist until that future time when all undesirables had been destroyed. The problem was that Nazis had so many on their list who were guilty of something: labor organizers, political opponents, critics of Nazi policies, and last, but not least, racial "subhumans." At first, the plan was to work inmates until they dropped dead, not to execute them.

The Nazis were not the first to try isolating large groups into camps. The Spanish did it during the Cuban Civil War, and the British did it in South Africa during the Boer War. In those cases, the purpose was to keep farmers from helping the rebels; because of poor sanitation, many died. POWs in nineteenth-century wars and the First World War suffered from unhealthy conditions and lack of food, but the purpose for holding them was to keep them from returning to their armies.

In the Nazi case, making people suffer was the *primary* reason for the bad conditions. From the beginning, the Nazis had drawn in cruel people, and Hitler could keep their support only by giving them a chance to work off their energy. After Hitler came to power, the SA began grabbing opponents, taking them to one of their 50 camps, and working them over. If the people were wealthy or had rich relatives and friends, they might be released after bribes had been paid. Even Nazi prosecutors complained about the torture, but the evils of those camps did not disturb Hitler. He said: "We must be ruthless. Only thus shall we purge our people of their softness."

After the purge of the SA, the SS took charge of constructing and running concentration camps. The first three were Dachau (near Munich), Buchenwald (near Weimar), and Sachsenhausen (near Berlin). When those became overcrowded, more were built. Some concentration camps were later turned into death camps.

No one in their right mind would ever wish to be sent to *any* of the camps, but some were worse than others. Even from the outside, they looked grim: barbed wire, guard towers, and unpainted buildings. At Dachau, Theodor Eicke was named commandant of the camp in 1933. More than anyone else, he set the tone not only for Dachau, but for every other camp. Many of the camp commanders began their careers at Dachau and copied his system in their camps. He demanded complete obedience from officers and guards; no one with a conscience could work there; he said anyone with a soft heart would be wise "to retire quickly to a monastery."

Prisoners were rarely taken directly to a prison camp. They were often kept in holding areas (jails, forts, stables, etc.) for days or weeks with little food or water. After they were physically and mentally weakened, they were marched, taken on a bus with covered windows, or trucked to a railroad station. Then, they were put on an overcrowded boxcar. They would be moved around several days before being delivered to the camp. After bombings began, the trains sometimes took very long routes to get past breaks in the line, but no matter how difficult transporting prisoners became, nothing stopped them from being delivered.

ARRIVAL. By the time the trip was over (it had often taken several days), the prisoners were very hungry and thirsty. Their dignity had been taken from them by the loss of privacy and by having to use buckets to relieve themselves. They were scared, as anyone would be in their situation.

As the train pulled in to be unloaded, the arrivals were lined up facing guards with muzzled dogs. As they marched into the camp, an orchestra composed of young girls often played light music to ease fears. A sorting process took place as a person in a white coat pointed the arrivals toward the left or right. The line they were sent to meant life or death. Those strong enough to work entered life in the concentration camp; the others were to be killed.

Those allowed to live were processed. An identification number was tatooed on the arm. An SS guard told one prisoner the purpose of the number was to "dehumanize" him. The prisoner was referred to afterward only by number. Then all the prisoner's hair was cut off. The hair was added to the huge piles already taken, and it was sold by the government to industries to use in coats, socks, mattress stuffing, ropes, and bomb mechanisms.

The first inmates were Communists and Jews, but other groups soon joined them. Each class of prisoners was identified by a badge on their shirt and pants. The color system was: red (political), purple (Jehovah's Witness), black (anti-social), green (criminal), pink (homosexual), brown (gypsy), and yellow triangles forming a Star of David (Jew). Foreigners were identified by "F" if French, "P" if Polish. The mentally defective had "Blöd" (stupid) written on theirs. No inmates were treated like humans, but the worst treatment was given to gypsies, Jews, and homosexuals.

Barracks were dark, gloomy, smelly, and overcrowded. At Auschwitz, inmates slept on wooden shelves with each allowed a space equal to that in a coffin. Plagued by hunger, filth, bitter cold in winter, and exhausting work in summer heat, most of their effort now was devoted to staying alive another day. Long hours of work, sometimes at useful jobs in factories, but often at senseless work in quarries, filled the days.

ACTIVITY:

Have students discuss why they think inmates were forced to wear colored badges. Then divide the class into three groups identified by red, white, or blue badges. Students should wear their badges for one day and take note of what happens. Do students wearing the same badges stick together? Do they pick on members of the other groups? Why or why not?

Name _____ Date _____

Challenges

1. When did most Western nations stop torturing prisoners?_____

_____

2. Who were some groups in German prisons that would not be considered criminals in most

other countries? _____

_____

3. Why did the English build camps during the Boer War? _____

_____

4. Who were the first in Nazi Germany to hold prisoners? _____

5. List the first three concentration camps run by the SS. _____

_____

6. What was Theodor Eicke's job? _____

_____

7. Why was the man with a white coat important to those arriving? _____

_____

8. What were tattooed onto the arms of inmates? _____

_____

9. If an inmate wore a red triangle with "F" on it, what could you tell about him? _____

_____

10. Who got the worst abuse in the concentration camps? _____

_____

Points to Consider

1. Do you think there was any reason for the prisoners to be taken on long rides before they arrived at the camps?
2. What would the combination of muzzled dogs and an orchestra playing do to your mind if you
were coming to the camp?
3. Do you think the badge system might cause groups of prisoners to dislike each other, or perhaps think they were better than some other group? How would that help the guards?

The Major Concentration Camps

From the beginning, Hitler's goal of ridding Germany of undesirables led to building concentration camps where they could be isolated. The first, Dachau, became the model for the others, and other camp commanders were often taught their jobs by Dachau's master, Theodor Eicke. Between 1934 and 1939, approximately 200,000 prisoners were sent to the camps; after the war began, their numbers increased rapidly.

DACHAU. Located near Munich, it was built to hold 8,000 prisoners, but it soon became overcrowded. Eicke, its commandant from 1933 to 1940, set the tone of the camp. Hanging offenses

Even children were imprisoned and killed in German concentration camps.

included inciting speeches, supplying atrocity stories to the opposition, and collecting true or untrue information and concealing it, talking about it, or smuggling it outside the camp. Anyone physically attacking a guard, refusing to obey an order, or giving speeches while marching or at work was shot on the spot or hanged later. Any remark critical of Nazi leaders or glorifying Communists or any liberal pre-Nazi leader was punished with 25 lashes and two weeks of solitary confinement.

Eicke's phrase, *"Arbeit macht frei"* (Work makes you free), hung over the entrance at Dachau and many other camps. The phrase became a mockery of camp realities, but when it was first used, Eicke thought prisoners would be released after they learned the error of their ways. In the early days, wealthy prisoners were released after a bribe had been paid, and some with visas allowing them to enter other countries left after signing papers saying they had not been mistreated. The policy soon changed, however. Himmler and other SS officials decided those who entered the camps as prisoners would never leave alive.

The guards, mostly Bavarian peasants, wore their Death's Head emblems proudly. They hated anyone who appeared intellectual (by wearing glasses, for instance), and all Jewish prisoners. The camp had all classes of prisoners mixed in together: anti-Nazi ministers like Dr. Niemöller, Communists, gypsies, alcoholics, criminals, and Jews. Every group there had some other group who did not like them and would turn them in to the guards. A prisoner could not even avoid cruelty at night, because the SS put long-time criminals in charge of the barracks.

Other concentration camps were similar in purpose and methods, but a few examples will give some insight into life in the camps.

VUGHT. In comparison with other camps, women had it easy at Vught, a camp in Holland. Prisoners wore blue overalls with a red stripe down the leg. The day began with prisoners standing at parade attention at 4 a.m. At 5:30, they had a breakfast of black bread and a drink resembling coffee. At 6 a.m., skilled workers were at work in a factory on the prison grounds, making radio parts for German aircraft. There was a one-hour break for a lunch of gruel made from wheat and peas. At 6 p.m., there was a roll call. Male prisoners had a much harder time than women.

THERESIENSTADT was an unusual camp built 35 miles north of Prague. The 7,000 Czechs who lived there were ordered out in 1941, and the Nazis turned it into a ghetto for the elderly, World War I veterans, and Jewish government officials who had been fired. They were soon joined by Czechs, Poles, and Dutch prisoners. It had a lending library, orchestra, lectures, schools, and an artist studio. In preparation for a visit by the Swedish Red Cross, buildings were painted, a restaurant was opened, and a soccer match was played. After the Swedes left, conditions dropped to normal.

Inmates of the art studio drew art that pleased the German masters by day; at night, they secretly drew pictures showing the hunger and bad treatment in the camp. These pictures were hidden and survived the Holocaust. In 1944, the camp became a shipping point for prisoners on their way to Auschwitz and death.

BERGEN-BELSEN was on the road to Hamburg. Opening in 1943, it quickly earned a reputation as one of the worst camps. Its commander, Josef Kramer (the "beast of Belsen"), totally ignored health and sanitation conditions. Cruelty was ordinary there; men with hands tied behind their backs were hung suspended for hours at a time. Prisoners were picked at random to be burned alive at the crematorium.

Inmates did not have to be killed to die, however. Starvation and disease were widespread. A typhus epidemic in 1944 killed thousands.

BUCHENWALD, a camp located near Weimar, was opened in 1933. Those who liberated the camp described the conditions that had killed thousands there. Neatly stacked piles of corpses lay unburied around the camp. Inmates starved on a daily diet of a piece of brown bread with a little margarine on top and a little stew. Death came by starvation, beatings, torture, and sickness. In a stable built for 80 horses, 1,200 men were housed. Inmates worked 12-hour shifts at a factory making guns and ammunition.

MAUTHAUSEN was one of the worst camps. Jews sent there worked in the stone quarry carrying heavy rocks up a steep slope. Many were crushed to death as they slipped while pushing heavy carts up the path. Some gave up hope and jumped off the ledge. Guards sometimes pushed inmates off the ledge, but that was stopped because non-prisoners who worked there complained about the mess.

The commandant, Franz Ziereis, was called "Babyface" by the prisoners, but there was nothing soft about him. Shootings, gassings, hangings, lethal injections, and torture by blasts of cold water were common. About 36,000 executions were reported at the prison.

No prisoner in the camp was treated like a human; surviving in the camp required both luck and learning quickly the methods of staying alive.

ACTIVITY:

Have the students write a journal entry about their lives in a concentration camp.

Name _____ Date _____

Challenges

1. Who taught other camp commanders how to run concentration camps? _____

_____

2. How many prisoners came to the camps between 1934 and 1939? _____

_____

3. What was the punishment for smuggling information about Dachau to the outside world?

_____

4. What was the punishment for saying a Communist slogan? _____

_____

5. What did the sign: *"Arbeit macht frei"* mean in English? _____

_____

6. What time did prisoners eat breakfast at Vught? What did their breakfast consist of?

_____

7. Why was a restaurant opened and a soccer game played at Theresienstadt? _____

_____

8. What was the nickname of Josef Kramer? _____

9. How many men were housed in one horse stable at Buchenwald? _____

10. What work did inmates at Mauthausen do? _____

_____

Points to Consider

1. Why do you think they stopped releasing prisoners from Dachau?
2. If you were a prisoner working 12 hours a day and eating as little as they did, what do you think you would be like in a month?
3. Why did the Nazis go through the trouble of cleaning up Theresienstadt? What does this say about their concerns?

Survival in a Concentration Camp

It takes little imagination to think of what a concentration camp was like for a new arrival. Anything that had seemed important before was trivial now. This was a world with its own rules, and those who did not adjust quickly died. Elderly people and small children did not do well in this world, and they died quickly. There were also the walking dead, the "Moslems," who wore the blank stare of death on their faces. But there were others who survived years in the camps, keeping their minds and bodies together. These old-timers told newcomers the first three months were the test, and if you could survive them, you could make it through three years. The inmate's basic key to survival was to live through one day at a time.

Appearing too smart (even wearing glasses was evidence of being intellectual) or appearing stupid (signified by the word *Blöd* on the uniform) made the inmate a special target. Those wearing the pink identification badge of a homosexual, the brown badge of a gypsy, or the yellow triangle of the Jew were in for an especially hard time.

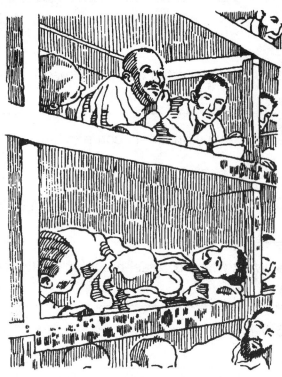

Around 1,200 men were crammed into a stable built to house 80 horses at the concentration camp at Buchenwald.

Nevertheless, about 700,000 out of the eight million sent to the camps survived. Those surviving years in the camps without losing their humanity were called the *Prominenten.* They were respected even by the guards. If they were talking to a new inmate, what advice might they give?

1. Don't cry. Before coming to the camp, you lost family security and endured humiliation and uncertainty. The time for crying is over. Now is the time of testing. To cry is a sign of weakness. No matter how tired you are or how unjust the punishment you endure, show no anger or self-pity.

2. Follow orders quickly. When they brought you into the camp, an officer told you: "Here you are not in a penitentiary or prison, but in a place of instruction. Order and discipline are the highest law here. If you ever want to see freedom again, you must submit to a severe training....Our methods are thorough! Here there is no compromise and no mercy....Here we sweep with an iron broom." Believe me, he meant it!

Don't argue with the guards and capos; they are quick to use their whips and clubs. Don't complain about the absurd things you are sometimes required to do. The roll calls can take hours. All the prisoners may be ordered to take caps off and put them on in unison for hours. You may spend a whole day lugging heavy stones to the right side of the road and the next day moving them to the left side of the road. Don't ask why.

3. Don't call attention to yourself. Resistance of any kind, even complaining, brings punishment on everyone else. If one person shows up late for roll call, the next roll call may last five or six hours, even if the temperature is -20°F. A mother scratched and bit an SS soldier who tried to separate her from her daughter. Both mother and daughter were shot, and the whole shipment was sent to be killed.

4. Try to look healthier than you feel. A selection process goes on continuously, and those who look like they have reached their limit are killed. Stuff rags or straw inside your uniform to look fatter than you are. You might prick a finger and smear blood on your face or massage your face to give it some color. They will make you trot around or make you run in place to prove you are healthy, even when every bone in your body is aching. If you want to stay alive, pass the test.

5. Find someone who can help you. Some work details are harder than others. Being assigned to the sewing room, the hospital, or a skilled labor job keeps you from being sent on hard labor details. Many camps have fine orchestras that play for officers and inmates. The competition for these is tough, and many of the musicians are professionals. They are allowed time off from other work details to practice and perform. Working at sorting clothing and jewelry at "Canada" (the storage room where articles taken from inmates are classified and stockpiled) gives you a chance to steal a little that might buy extra food from the guards.

A friendly clerk might save you. If your number is on the list of those to be gassed, he might substitute the number of someone who has died. A few contractors rent prisoners and save their lives by claiming these inmates are "essential personnel."

6. Become callous. Ignore the beating of the old man or young woman going on nearby. This is no time for personal dignity, concern about the quality of food, or standing up for rights. Don't be offended by the stench of the camp or the death all around you. Be careful about calls for volunteers to work on special projects. These sometimes involve harder work or some medical experiment they are wanting to perform.

Don't trust anyone too far. Some inmates have become nearly animals. Keep your eye on your cap, because anyone without a cap on during roll call is shot. Eat your food before someone steals it from you. Survival requires a toughness that doesn't exist in the world beyond the barbed wire fence.

7. Have a reason for living. They are trying to destroy your humanity, and the main thing separating the animal from the human is your ability to reason. Believe that God has a purpose for your life, and you must survive to fulfill that purpose. Believe in yourself, that you can and will outlast them. Survive so you can tell the story of what you and your family have suffered during these impossible times. Survive so you can tell the liberator about the cruelty of the guards and see them brought to justice.

Find ways to occupy your time. Some women talk about recipes, or men talk about the work they did or farm animals they used. Religion is secretly discussed by the inmates. There are rabbis and pastors who encourage others by reminding them that God rewards those who keep the faith and punishes those who abuse the innocent.

ACTIVITY:

The list included in this unit is not complete. From what you have learned in other units, what suggestions might you give for surviving?

Name _____ Date _____

Challenges

1. Who were the "Moslems"? _____

_____

2. What might make the guards think you were "intellectual"? _____

_____

3. Who were the Prominenten? _____

_____

4. What were inmates told were the highest laws of the camp? _____

_____

5. What punishment did other prisoners receive when one showed up late for roll call?

_____

6. What happened to inmates who appeared to have reached their limit? _____

_____

7. What was "Canada"? _____

_____

8. What should the inmate do when the person next to him or her was beaten? _____

_____

9. What should the inmate do when he or she received food? Why? _____

_____

10. Why should the inmate be careful about what he or she volunteered for? _____

_____

Points to Consider

1. What did the Prominenten mean when they told the new inmate that if you can survive the first three months, you can survive the next three years?

2. Which of these guides for survival would you have the most trouble carrying out?

3. If the camp was the "school" the Nazis said it was, what lessons were the "teachers" trying to get across to the "students"?

Murder Becomes Nazi Policy

The Nazis had never been nervous about killing. They had killed Communists in street battles, and the public approved. They had shot SA leaders, and most Germans were glad they were gone. They had always said Germany must rid itself of its "subhumans," political trouble makers, and mental and physical defectives. Unlike many in politics, they meant it.

EARLY PROGRAMS. In 1938, Hitler created a committee that was to decide whether children born with weak or deformed bodies should be allowed to live. A child not meeting their standards was to be taken to a hospital far from home for "the best and most modern therapy available." The child was given powerful medicine and then he or she slipped into a coma.

To eliminate the chronically ill or insane adult, the T4 program was created. Those to be killed were sent to converted mental hospitals in rural areas and were gassed with carbon monoxide. The family received a death certificate listing some fake cause of death and was assured that every effort to save their loved one had failed. A few weeks later, the cremated body was sent home in an urn.

SS General Reinhard Heydrich was the chairman of the Wannsee Conference.

It did not take long for T4 to become a scandal. One person received two urns each supposedly containing the body of the same person. A person who was listed as dying of appendicitis had had his appendix removed a few years before. Those who did the killing often talked about their jobs in taverns. Even Nazi doctors protested, and when ministers attacked T4 from the pulpit, Hitler called off the project temporarily.

To remove controversy over these policies, Goebbels attacked Jewish doctors. *Der Sturmer,* the anti-Semitic tabloid, warned Germans that the evil Jewish doctors were using medicines to destroy the Master Race.

Euthanasia is mercy killing. Many today believe a person with an incurable and terribly painful disease should have the right, *if they choose,* to be assisted in dying. The Nazi version of euthanasia was to help someone die if they were considered "better off dead." The patient was not consulted. Officials looking at reports made the decision to end a patient's life.

In early 1941, Himmler ordered that concentration camps get rid of "excess" prisoners. This program was called "14f13." The selection process began. A person criticizing Hitler was a "mental deficient." A Communist was an "anti-social psychopath." For the Jewish inmate, the only question was whether he could work. Any of these "excess" prisoners were put on the list for "special treatment" (death).

The job of deciding who was to go on the list was usually left to doctors who were prisoners themselves. The most obvious choices were the very elderly, those too young to work, and those in very poor health. If not enough could be found to fill the quota, other prisoners became "excess."

MEDICAL EXPERIMENTS were performed by Nazi doctors using inmates as guinea pigs. Inmates might be vaccinated with serum containing deadly diseases or dropped into icy water to see how long they could survive. The most notorious experiments were by Dr. Josef Mengele (called "the Angel of Death") and Dr. Heinz Thilo (called "the Devil of Death") at Auschwitz. Mengele looked for prisoners who were twins to find a way to multiply the Master Race. He experimented on inmates with eyes of different colors, and he even tried to create Siamese twins. His experiments were as cruel as they were worthless.

FINAL SOLUTION. The Nazis rarely called any of their cruel programs by their real names. Instead, they found words like "final solution," "total solution," and "solution possibility" as substitutes for the reality of the mass murder of Jews and other "subhumans." In July 1941, SD chief Heydrich was given the green light to wipe out all of Europe's Jews. He faced big problems. (1) To transport prisoners to death camps strained the transportation system, and trains were needed for military purposes. (2) Getting rid of bodies was a problem. In the past, they had buried bodies, but during spring thaws, the bodies had come back to the surface. More incinerators were needed to dispose of bodies. (3) Shooting prisoners was hard on the guards, and many had become alcoholics or suffered mental breakdowns. Some way was needed that saved bullets and was not so hard on the killers. (4) Bad publicity might hurt public morale. Too many photographs had been taken at killing sites, and upset soldiers had written descriptions of what they had seen. (5) There were some Nazi officials who thought it was foolish to kill a Jew when his labor was needed for the war effort. What good was a dead Jew? Heydrich argued that the destruction of Jews was as necessary as winning battles. The destruction of Jews took priority over army needs. Hitler agreed with Heydrich's view, and gave him the power to act.

WANNSEE CONFERENCE. To discuss the problems of carrying out the total destruction of Europe's Jews, Heydrich called a meeting in the Berlin suburb of Wannsee. Scheduled for December 8, 1941, it was postponed until January 20, 1942. Officials from the Eastern regions, the economic and justice departments, the foreign office, SS, and RSHA were present. Heydrich informed the others that Hitler had approved removing Jews from Germany and sending them east as a "solution possibility." Many were expected to die of natural causes on the trip, but those surviving were the real menace because if they lived beyond the war, they might revive Jewish culture.

Heydrich read off the numbers of Jews to be killed: 131,800 German; 5 million Russian; 865,000 French; 742,000 Hungarian; etc. A Nazi official suggested that the Final Solution begin in Poland, since Jews there would not have to be transported. Heydrich and Himmler had already decided to begin the killing in Poland and had started building six death camps there.

The meeting was interrupted by lunch, and after they had eaten, they discussed the best methods for killing. Heydrich was pleased with the enthusiasm all had shown for his project.

ACTIVITY:
To get some idea of how many Jews were killed by the Nazis, have the class take a map of the United States, and find a city of comparable size to those executed in: Austria - 50,000; Latvia - 71,500; Lithuania - 143,000; Netherlands - 143,000; Poland - 3 million; Rumania - 287,000; Russia - 1.1 million; Hungary - 569,000. Mark that American city off the map.

Name _____ Date _____

Challenges

1. What were parents told about the care their weak or deformed child was to receive? _____
_____

2. What was the purpose of T4? _____
_____

3. How were victims of T4 killed? _____
_____

4. What was the victim's family told about the death? _____
_____

5. What was Hitler's reaction to protests against T4? _____
_____

6. What was the difference between Nazi euthanasia and the usual use of the word? _____
_____

7. What problem had shooting prisoners caused for guards? _____
_____

8. Who were two German doctors performing medical experiments? _____
_____

9. What was meant by "Final Solution." _____
_____

10. Where was the meeting held to discuss the Final Solution? Who was in charge at the meeting?
_____

Points to Consider

1. How would programs like killing weak children or chronically ill adults seem perfectly logical to the Nazis?

2. Considering all the problems facing the Final Solution, what does the decision to go ahead with it tell you about the Nazis.

3. The Wannsee Conference was kept secret from the public. How do you think Germans might have reacted if they had learned of it?

Death Camps

The Nazis were fighting two wars at the same time: one against the Allies, and one to destroy the "subhuman races." Of the two, the war against the races was usually given priority. In 1944 and 1945, trains that could have carried supplies to the army fighting for its life in Russia carried Jews to their deaths in Poland. It seems that hating was more important than winning.

A crematorium

Death camps had a different purpose than concentration camps. Concentration camps focused on getting work done for industry; the inmates produced until they died. Death camps were less practical; their main purpose was to kill as quickly as pos-sible, although some had a small work camp. Many prisoners moved directly from the train to the shower room for gassing, then to the crematorium where their bodies were burned.

The death camps were the end result of the process that had begun with *Einsatzgruppen* units killing Russian Jews. The Wannsee Conference in January 1942 had focused on better ways to kill. The Master Race was to be built on the ashes of the innocent.

Their approach was very organized. The clothing of those killed was disinfected, valuables were sorted, and victims' hair was shaved and then collected. The bodies were removed from the showers, "dentists" removed gold and platinum fillings from the teeth, bodies were disposed of, and the "shower room" cleaned for the next group.

Expenses were kept to the minimum. The staff of guards was very small, and the few inmates were *Sonderkommandos* who had the dirty work of body disposal. Food for the inmates was the main cost. Jewish inmates received a turnip soup for lunch and supper; bread mixed with sawdust and margarine, old sausage, and what passed for marmalade was served for breakfast. Unpuri-fied water caused epidemics that killed thousands.

The JANOWSKI camp outside Lwow, Poland, was a good example of the smaller death camps. Inmates suffered constant hunger and terrible overcrowding. After a hard day's work, they were forced to run through the camp; those unable to survive the test were shot. Inmates too ill to work were forced to dig their own graves and lie in them, waiting to be shot.

The larger extermination camps were all in Poland. They were all similar, but a brief view of each gives the picture.

CHELMNO was located near the Polish district town of Kolo. An old castle was the center of the operation. When prisoners arrived by truck, they were told they were going to be resettled in Germany, but before they went, they were to shower. After removing their clothes, they were herd-ed into vans, where they were gassed by carbon monoxide.

TREBLINKA was located northeast of Warsaw; it began operation in 1942, and in its first year, it took 800,000 lives. A railroad station similar to those in Germany was built there. New arrivals undressed and were led down "the Way to Heaven" (*Himmelstrasse*) to the showers. Prisoners were told that after showering, they would be classified by trades, so most went quietly to their deaths. Others were less willing and had to be driven with whips. None survived the gassing with carbon monoxide. Later, Zyklon-B, a pesticide, was used.

The first commander at Treblinka was Dr. Irmfried Ebert, a physician and devoted Nazi. His mistake of leaving exposed bodies near the railroad station left no doubt for Jews as to what awaited them. Rumors about Treblinka reached the Warsaw Ghetto, so now the Jews knew what "resettlement opportunities" announced by the Germans really meant. With a capacity of about 15,000, this was one of the largest death camps. Yet, its staff was only about 24 Germans, guards from conquered Baltic countries, and Jewish *Sonderkommandos.* It was an efficient machine of death. Nearly everyone sent there was dead within a few hours.

SOBIBOR. A prisoner orchestra played for those who came, but the only other music there was the screaming of those being gassed. There was no pretense of it being a work camp. No selection took place. The prisoner population numbered only about 1,000 inmates, and they did the dirty work. After the new arrivals were gassed, their bodies were burned in open trenches.

MAJDANEK was outside Lublin and was used for Russian POWs, Polish political prisoners, and Jews. The guards there enjoyed making inmates suffer. Mothers were forced to watch as their small children were killed. Inmates were forced to put on and take off hats in rhythm for hours at a time. During roll calls, prisoners were called out and hanged. Russian POWs held there froze or starved to death. Of 200,000 who died at Majdanek, about 125,000 were Jews.

BELZEC, also near Lublin, began as a concentration camp, but it became a death camp in 1942. Its first commander was Odilo Globocnik, who also founded Sobibor and Majdanek. The killing business at Belzec began with a sergeant gassing prisoners with a diesel engine and carbon monoxide. However, the system was deemed too slow and unreliable. The pesticide Zyklon-B was first tested on humans at Belzec, and thereafter it became the standard method used in extermination camps. An estimated 600,000 Jews and 2,000 Poles died there.

STUTTHOFF, near Danzig, was established in 1939. Beginning as a concentration camp for Norwegian inmates, its purpose shifted in 1941 when Jews were transferred there from overcrowded Auschwitz. Most died from freezing and starving rather than gassing. Inmates were delivered to Stutthoff on slow barges. The trip of 14 miles took three days. One shipment of Jews was given no water and only 10 ounces of bread per person for the trip.

In 1945, as the Russian army came closer, the Jews were marched from the camp in a driving snowstorm. One group was forced to walk out into ice cold water, and they were shot if they tried to return to land.

ACTIVITY:

At Sobibor, a young inmate was put to work sorting out the clothes of those who had gone to the gas chamber. He found the clothes of his brother in the pile. Imagine you were him and try to write a diary entry or a poem about the experience.

Name _____ Date _____

Challenges

1. What was more important to Hitler: winning the war or killing "subhuman" races? _____

_____

2. What was the job of the *Sonderkommando*? _____

_____

3. What food was given to Jewish *Sonderkommandos*? _____

_____

4. What happened to inmates at Janowski who were too ill to work? _____

_____

5. How were inmates at Chelmno killed? _____

_____

6. What mistake did Dr. Ebert make at Treblinka? _____

_____

7. How many Germans were stationed at Treblinka? _____

8. How many inmates worked at Sobibor? _____

9. Where was Zyklon-B first used on prisoners? _____

_____

10. How much food were inmates given for the three-day barge trip to Stutthoff? _____

_____

Points to Consider

1. Why were death camps considered to be necessary by the Nazis in completing their Final Solution?

2. What effect do you think being a guard at a death camp would have on a person's personality?

3. Why were the Germans so anxious to destroy the death camps before the Russian army arrived?

Auschwitz

An inmate described Auschwitz as "hell on earth." A Nazi might have described it as the largest camp, serving as both a concentration and death camp. In size and evil, nothing ever devised could match it. Located 160 miles from Warsaw in a marshland with few Poles living nearby, it had the virtues of good railroad facilities and abundant coal. I.G. Farben Co. was interested in building a synthetic fuel plant there. With Russian POWs and Polish captives to do the work, there would be no shortage of inmates to work to death.

The words over the gate to the main camp at Auschwitz mean "Work makes free."

The commander at Auschwitz in the early days was Rudolf Hoess. A true believer in the SS motto of "Believe! Obey! Fight!", he had joined the Frei Korps in the 1920s and the SS in 1934. He was noted for loving animals, but he turned a blind eye to the prisoner's needs. He operated the camp without the restraint of conscience. He was "just doing his duty."

The SS officer in charge of prisoners, Karl Fritsch, said: "If there are Jews in the transport, they don't have the right to live more than two weeks; priests, one month, and the others, three months."

The first prisoners at Auschwitz were "dangerous Poles" (intellectuals, Communists, and Jews). An SS officer told them: "You have come not to a sanitorium here, but to a German concentration camp, and the only way out is through the chimney of the crematorium." Escapes were rare; when the first occurred, prisoners were forced to stand at attention 20 straight hours. Those accused of aiding the escape were tortured. After another escape, 10 prisoners were taken to a cellar, where they starved to death.

Across from Auschwitz was another camp called Birkenau, built for 100,000 Russian POWs. To provide for all these prisoners, more barracks were built, but never enough. To meet the needs for housing, Himmler reduced the space allowed for each inmate. In a barracks built for 550, there were 750 prisoners. Toilet barracks were built, but inmates had only 10 to 15 minutes a day to use them. At other times, waste buckets in the housing barracks were used. When the bucket was full, a prisoner had to carry it to the toilets for disposal.

From the beginning, it was assumed that prisoners would die in large numbers. A contract for a crematorium was signed with J.A. Topf & Sons before the first prisoner arrived. By 1943, the camp had one incinerator that could dispose of 340 bodies each day, two to handle 1,440 each, and two to handle 768 each, a total of 4,756 bodies per day.

The number sent to Auschwitz is estimated at as few as 1.1 million and as high as four million. Many of the arrivals were not even listed on the records; they were sent to be destroyed immediately. Hungarian Jews were the largest single group; 438,000 were sent in the summer of 1944 alone. About 300,000 Polish Jews were sent, along with lesser numbers from other conquered lands.

SELECTION was a dreaded process that began with arrival at the camp. As soon as the train stopped and the doors of the cattle cars opened, the guards shouted: "*Raus! Raus!* (Hurry! Hurry!)". Men were separated from women and children. Then all passed by an SS doctor who motioned to the left (life at hard labor) or the right (death). Those most likely to be gassed were the elderly, mothers with small children, and pregnant women. Families were split up in emotional scenes in front of impatient guards. Both columns were told to leave their belongings and promised they would be returned later. As soon as they left, capos opened the luggage and began sorting out the contents, which were dumped in large piles: watches, jewelry, etc. All of this now became the property of the German government. Watches and fountain pens were given as Christmas presents to SS troops and wounded soldiers; clothing was sent to poor Germans.

Those allowed to live had their heads shaved, were tattooed, and were sent to a barrack. Each day, the selection process continued, as doctors looked for patients who did not look healthy. Those judged to be sick might be sent to the hospital; if they did not recover within two days, they were gassed. When workers came in from work, they were made to run to prove they were in good enough condition to live another day. The meager rations caused typhus epidemics to sweep through the barracks.

WORK was part of the routine at the camp. Many worked at the Farben plant or in one of the factories on the grounds. A few jobs were much preferred over the others. A prisoner orchestra made up of pretty girls in nice uniforms played as workers went to their jobs and returned.

Being assigned to "Canada" was an opportunity to live longer. The inmates sorting through the large piles often stole small items, which they traded with corrupt guards for food. The amount stored there was enormous. Before leaving, the Germans burned 29 of the 35 warehouses in Canada. In the remaining six, the Russians found more than a million suits, coats, and dresses, seven tons of human hair, and huge heaps of shoes, eyeglasses, and cooking utensils.

There were certain parts of the camp where one did not want to be. Block 10 was where medical experiments were conducted. Block 11 was the jail. Block 20 was the hospital where people were killed. The "black wall" was where prisoners were shot, and hangings were at the gallows.

DEATH. In September 1941, the gassing of prisoners began on a large scale, with 900 Russian POWs being used in the experiment. The prisoners were given soap and towels and led to the "shower." When the gas poured in, the prisoners beat on the doors, but they held. Hoess was pleased with his success, especially since he knew many Jews were going to be sent there.

By the end of its operation, Auschwitz was killing 6,000 a day. Record-keeping fell behind, but one day in 1943 gives an example. On January 19, 1943, 164 men and 134 women were admitted as prisoners; the 1,702 others in the shipment were killed in the gas chamber. One expert believes that 1.3 million entered the camp, and 1.1 million of those died.

ACTIVITY:

Read to the class portions of Elie Wiesel's *Night*. An especially effective section might be his introduction to Auschwitz (pp. 35–37). Ask for student comments on that experience.

Name _____ Date _____

Challenges

1. Why was Auschwitz chosen as the site for a concentration camp? _____

_____

2. Who was its first commander? _____

3. Who did the Nazis consider to be "dangerous Poles"? _____

_____

4. What kind of prisoner was Birkenau built for? _____

_____

5. How many bodies a day could be incinerated? _____

6. What prisoners were most likely to be immediately gassed? _____

_____

7. What was done with watches and fountain pens? _____

_____

8. How long was a sick person allowed to recover? _____

9. Why was "Canada" a good place to work? _____

_____

_____

10. What was the "black wall"? _____

_____

Points to Consider

1. How would fellow prisoners react if they knew you were planning an escape from Auschwitz?

2. Some argue that Auschwitz was never a death camp. What arguments could you give that it was?

3. Why were the Nazis so generous in giving away presents from the goods gathered at Auschwitz? How would you react if you knew where they had come from?

The Ghettos

To understand why Jews went to live in the ghettos without much resistance, one needs to keep several things in mind.

Jews were rounded up and forced to move into ghettos.

1. Ghettos were not a new invention. They had existed as far back as the Middle Ages. In the nineteenth century, Jews had been confined to certain parts of cities or required to live "beyond the Pale" in rural areas of Eastern Europe. Being separated by the Germans was nothing new.

2. Few Jews owned guns or had officer training in military strategy. This made it difficult to organize an armed resistance.

3. Community and family were very strong in Jewish culture. Most Jews followed the advice of leaders who trusted reason as the way to convince the Nazis. They argued: "What good is a dead Jew to them?" They believed the Germans needed Jews to work in their factories. They also knew the SS swiftly punished disobedience. They thought that by cooperating with the SS, their masters would ease up on the pressure.

Family was very important. To be with relatives in uncertain times was important to survival. Parents often gave their food ration to their children. When families were transported to labor camps, mothers often gave up their own lives by staying with the children, and they went to die with them.

4. The Jews were too scattered in isolated *shtetls* and in small clusters in Gentile cities to put up effective resistance.

THE ORDER TO MOVE to the ghetto came with little warning. The *shtetl* leaders might be told early in the morning to have the Jews assembled and ready to move by 9 a.m. They could take only a suitcase or a small handcart. Some hid valuables, but their homes, furniture, and livestock had to be left behind. At the appointed time, they moved out, and scavengers quickly descended to steal whatever they could find.

Their column might join others headed for the ghetto. There, new arrivals were assigned a room. In an apartment where a family of four had lived before, 12 to 20 lived now. There was no privacy, few toilets, and little food. People were the only thing not in short supply. The streets were filled with beggars, the unemployed, and merchants selling smuggled food.

The Germans intended to make life for these "subhumans" as miserable and short as possible. Despite all the odds, Jews began to develop a system of schools, newspapers, and cultural and religious organizations. Schools were secretly organized, and students studied harder than ever before. Underground libraries sprang up, with the librarian secretly bringing books to the reader and picking them up. There were performances by ghetto orchestras before audiences starved for culture as well as food.

Religious life went on despite Nazi efforts to stop it. Many who had never been religious before took Judaism seriously now. Conditions in which they lived complicated Jewish law, and rabbis had to consider new issues. Such questions as whether it was permitted to wear the clothes of someone who had died or whether one could eat non-Kosher food were considered. The rabbis ruled that preserving life was more important than dietary law.

GOVERNMENT of the ghetto was done by the *Judenrat,* which took orders from the Nazis. The leaders faced a thankless task, since those who told them what they must do had no interest in helping them create a pleasant community for those who lived there. The situations in Lodz, Warsaw, and Kovno illustrate different approaches to their task.

Lodz. The leader of the Lodz ghetto was Mordechai Rumkowski, who wanted to keep the Nazis happy at all costs. No food was to be smuggled in. As many workers as the Germans wanted were sent on labor details. Everyone was required to work; many were employed at one of the council's factories. Rumkowski believed that if the ghetto was productive, the Nazis would leave it alone. When other ghettoes were being destroyed, the Lodz ghetto was allowed to continue, but its future was bleak.

In 1942, the Nazis began "resettling" Lodz Jews, sending them to Chelmno death camp. When the Nazis ordered Rumkowski to turn over the old people and children, he told parents to give him their sons and daughters. Many parents hid their children, but the Germans came into the ghetto and took them. After that, the Nazis left the Lodz ghetto alone for two years, then demanded more residents to be taken to Auschwitz and Chelmno. In August 1944, Rumkowski was taken and killed at Auschwitz.

Warsaw had the largest ghetto, with 400,000 Jews at its peak. The top man was Adam Czerniakow, a long-time leader of Warsaw's Jews. He made little effort to stop smuggling into the ghetto, and smugglers and children worked their way through sewers and holes under the wall to gather food for the residents. Smugglers charged high prices for food they brought in and lived much better than their customers.

In 1942, the Germans began taking Jews from the ghetto by quick attacks on blocks or buildings. Those captured were shipped to Treblinka. Czerniakow begged the Germans to let children go free; when he was turned down, he committed suicide.

Kovno in Lithuania had been a center for Jewish culture, but the city's Jewish population had suffered since the Russians took it in 1939. The Germans captured the city in 1941, and anti-Semitic Lithuanians killed 10,000 Jews in the first month of German occupation. The 30,000 remaining Jews were sealed off in a ghetto. The head of its *Judenrat* was Dr. Elchanan Elkes, who did his best to protect his people. In 1943, Dr. Elkes was taken away. By 1945, only 2,000 Jews were still alive in Kovno.

By 1943, the Nazis were determined to bring the Final Solution to a close. The only choice for those still surviving in the ghettos was whether to fight or die.

ACTIVITY:

The class becomes a *Judenrat,* and you have to make the following decisions:

1. The Nazis want 1,000 people per day to be resettled. Who would you choose?

2. The people are complaining that wealthy people are smuggling food while others starve. Should you crack down on smuggling?

3. Some young people want the council to give them money to buy guns. Should you spend council funds on guns?

4. Musicians have scheduled a concert and have asked for an extra ration of bread each as their pay. Should it be given?

Name _____ Date _____

Challenges

1. When had the first ghettos been established? _____

_____

2. When would *shtetl* leaders be told to prepare their people to move? _____

_____

3. What happened when they moved out? _____

_____

4. What were some signs of "normal life" in the ghetto? _____

_____

_____

5. What was the only thing in the ghetto not in short supply? _____

6. Who did the *Judenrat* answer to? _____

_____

7. What policy did Rumkowski use at Lodz? _____

_____

8. When the Nazis wanted the children of the ghetto, what did Rumkowski do? _____

_____

9. What did Czerniakow do when the Nazis demanded he give up the children? _____

_____

10. Who killed the Jews of Kovno in the first month after the Germans came? _____

_____

Points to Consider

1. Why did the Nazis give the Jews so little time to prepare to move?
2. Why do you think students were so anxious to attend classes?
3. What reason might one leader give for not allowing smuggling, and why would another ignore it?

Jewish Resistance

The Wannsee Conference had made the death of every Jew a priority in Nazi-occupied Europe. Any Jew who succeeded in living was defying Hitler's policy. So even the Jew who did not wear his yellow badge, did not register with a *Judenrat*, and mixed in with the general public was resisting. In Eastern Europe, some Jewish families sneaked out of the *shtetl* or ghetto and escaped to the woods. Small groups of these refugees

Although most Jews tried to live by the Nazi's rules, resistance came in various forms, from hiding to participating in uprisings to just staying alive.

lived a lonely and dangerous life, ever fearful of being spotted. These groups often included mothers with young children and elderly men. They could not stay anywhere too long, and during the day, they could not build a fire because an informer or airplane flying overhead might spot them.

The vast majority of Jews lived by the Nazi's rules, hoping that the Germans would realize they were useful labor for the war. In Eastern Europe, millions had been forced to leave their homes and move to the ghettos. There, they endured misery beyond imagination. They either believed they were being "relocated" when they boarded the cattle car that took them to the death camp, or they were too exhausted and no longer cared.

Others were unwilling to give in so quietly; if they were going to die, some German was going with them. A Lithuanian Jew, Abba Kovner, warned other young people not to be tricked by the Nazis; people of the ghetto were not being sent on labor details or even to concentration camps. They were going to the slaughter. "Brothers! It is better to die fighting like free men than to live at the mercy of the murderers." Those resisting included those joining partisan units and participating in concentration camp and ghetto uprisings.

PARTISANS joined armed groups resisting the German occupation. Some units were all Jewish, some all Gentile, and some were mixed. Gentile bands could be as anti-Semitic as the Germans, so the Jew had to be careful when approaching any band. Partisans operated in small units and raided German camps, supply lines, and communications. In Yugoslavia, 2,000 Jews joined Tito's army, which fought the Germans and their cruel Yugoslav allies, the Ustashi. In Italy, from 2,000 to 3,000 Jews joined the resistance. In France, they helped other Jews escape and were active in the French resistance.

CONCENTRATION CAMP UPRISINGS. Who is weaker than a beaten and starved prisoner known only by the number on his tattoo? The Nazis had killed many potential leaders, and they had spies among the inmates who were willing to turn in their own mothers for a potato. Despite the odds, uprisings were planned and carried out at a few camps.

In 1943, at *Treblinka,* prisoners began collecting anything that might be useful in fighting. They got a break when an armory door was brought to the workshop for repair; the inmates made a mold of the lock and made a key. About 60 men were involved in a plot to kill some guards and escape into the woods. Armed with hand grenades, pistols, rifles, shovels, and pickaxes, they attacked in August. After setting fire to the crematoria and fake railroad station, they headed for the forest. A few were never captured, but those caught were killed.

At *Sobibor,* a daring escape was led by a Russian Jew in October 1943. By nightfall, over half of the inmates escaped into the forest a few yards away. About one-third were recaptured, and many others froze in the cold Polish winter. Only a few are known to have survived. Two days after the uprising, Himmler ordered that the camp be destroyed.

At *Birkenau,* a group of Sonderkommandos persuaded women inmates working at the munitions factory to smuggle explosives to them. In October 1944, their revolt began. Some SS and Capos were killed, and the inmates broke through the fence. A massive manhunt found all of the men, and they were tortured and killed. The four women were hanged.

GHETTO UPRISINGS were difficult to carry out because many in the ghetto feared the Nazis so much they did not want anyone to do anything that might make conditions worse. But the time came when it was clear the Nazis were going to kill every Jew in the ghetto, and then, many were willing to go down fighting. In many ghettos in Eastern Europe, groups secretly organized to fight. The uprising in Warsaw is the most famous.

The *Warsaw Ghetto* had been shrinking in population since the death camp at Auschwitz had gone into operation. Jews from Lublin had told how the Nazis had destroyed the ghetto there, but the Warsaw *Judenrat* did not believe them. When the Nazis demanded that the *Judenrat* supply 8,000 people each day for "relocation," many realized the ghetto was doomed. By 1943, the once overcrowded ghetto was down to 65,000. For the ZOB in Warsaw, they must resist now or never.

The ZOB made contact with the Polish underground. The Poles sold them a few guns they had, but far from enough to win a battle with the Waffen SS. The Poles also sent reports of German troop movements to them. In April 1943, the Poles warned the ZOB the German attack would be soon. On April 19, troops marched into the ghetto, but they were beaten back by the Jewish defenders—something they had never dreamed possible. The ZOB had few illusions they were actually going to win, but they fought to kill as many Nazi soldiers as possible and to prove Jews were not cowards. The Nazis shelled and burned buildings, flooded sewers, and cut off gas, electricity, and water. The revolt's leader, Mordechai Anielewicz, was killed May 8, and by May 15, only occasional gunfire was heard. SS General Jurgen Stroop reported that his men had killed 13,000 to 14,000.

After the uprising, the ghetto's Jews were sent to death camps. One of those sent was Dr. Janusz Korczak, a popular radio personality. He had refused to escape in 1939 because the children of his orphanage needed him. When their time came to leave for Auschwitz, he dressed the children in their best clothes and walked beside them to their deaths.

ACTIVITY:

Your students are inmates of a concentration camp. Have them make a list of things they would need and another list of what they would need to know before they could make a successful escape. *If they have watched the movie, "The Great Escape," it might help.*

Name _____ Date _____

Challenges

1. Why was simply staying alive an act of rebellion? _____

_____

2. What did the term "relocation" really mean? _____

_____

3. Who were the partisans? _____

_____

4. Who were the Ustashi? _____

_____

5. How did the prisoners at Treblinka get a key to the armory? _____

_____

6. Why were the four women hanged at Auschwitz? _____

_____

7. Why were many ghetto residents reluctant to join a rebellion? _____

_____

8. Why did others join groups plotting uprisings? _____

_____

9. Who led the Warsaw uprising? _____

10. What happened to the Jews who survived the Warsaw uprising? _____

_____

Points to Consider

1. Why did some Jews choose not to wear the yellow badge and escape the ghetto? Would it be safer for them in a big city or rural area, among strangers or people they knew?

2. List problems concentration camp inmates had in planning and carrying out an uprising and escape.

3. Why might Dr. Korczak be considered a hero?

Rescuing Jews

In 1952, Israel created the Commission of Martyrs and Heroes to honor the "Righteous Among the Nations of the World." Its purpose was to honor those who had saved Jews during the Holocaust. To qualify, the person must have (1) been a non-Jew, (2) performed more than an act of charity, (3) not done it for personal gain, (4) been nominated by the person rescued, and (5) not done it at the last minute of the war to create a favorable impression.

Certainly, those who helped Jews during the war did not do it because they wanted an award afterward. The risks were great. Everyone knew what the Nazis did to those who helped Jews escape or hide. It was also known that the Germans punished not only the hider, but also the family, and perhaps everyone on their block. Saving Jews made the rescuer unpopular, not only among anti-Semites, but among others fearing for their lives. Still, individuals, groups, and even nations did it. Their courage and resourcefulness saved thousands of lives.

Raoul Wallenberg, a Swedish aristocrat, helped save thousands of Jews in Budapest, Hungary.

INDIVIDUALS. Many individuals helped Jews hide or escape. They hid them in attics, cellars, barns, haystacks, and sheds. They forged identity papers and baptismal certificates. They took in small children and raised them as their own. There were ministers, priests, monks, and nuns who sheltered Jews. Experts say that before a person will help someone in need, certain things happen. (1) They realize something is wrong, (2) they decide the person needs help, (3) they make it a personal duty to help, (4) they choose a way to help, and (5) then they carry out their plan.

Some helped in small ways. A Hungarian officer provided water and helped when his Jewish prisoners tired on a long march. An Italian policeman warned Jews he was scheduled to arrest them the next morning. Ministers and priests inserted baptismal records in their church files for Jews and hid Jews away. Of the individuals who helped Jews, two became famous for their efforts.

RAOUL WALLENBERG was a Swedish aristocrat with a diplomatic passport and an enthusiasm for saving as many Jews as possible. Arriving in Budapest, Hungary, in 1944, Wallenberg handed out official-looking diplomatic papers to thousands of Jews, even to Jews who were on convoys destined for death camps. He argued with many SS officials with such confidence that they backed down. He supplied drivers' licenses and forged documents for Jews without identity papers. At the end of the war, thousands of Hungarian Jews owed their lives to him.

OSKAR SCHINDLER was an unlikely hero. A Nazi party member, he enjoyed most vices known to man: drinking, adultery, greed, and opportunism among them. In 1942, he went to Krakow to open a factory using Polish Jews as his secret investors and slave laborers as his employees. He became dedicated to helping Jews escape the gas chamber. When asked later why he had done it, he replied: "If you saw a dog going to be crushed under a car, wouldn't you help him? Claiming his workers were vital for the war effort, he saved 1,200 from the gas chambers. He was not well-known, however, until Steven Spielberg's movie, *Schindler's List,* came out in 1993.

GROUPS. There were occasions when groups and even communities took the risk of helping Jews. LE CHAMBON was a Huguenot (Protestant) community of 5,000 only 40 miles from Vichy,

France. When Pastor André Trocme's wife found a Jewish woman shivering at her door one cold morning and invited her to come in, it was the beginning of an effort on the part of the town and the neighboring region to save Jews. At times, German troops recovering from wounds were stationed there, right across from a hotel where Jews were hidden away. When asked why they had helped, the people explained: "We were doing what had to be done. Who else could help them?"

ZEGOTA was a Catholic movement in Poland that provided hiding places, documents, food, medical care, and arms for the Jewish resistance. It is estimated that 100,000 Jews were saved by the group. The Zegota was very unpopular with many Poles, and joining was very risky. In one district alone, 210 Zegota members were executed.

NATIONS. Some nations protected their Jews better than others. Among those with the highest percentage of Jews killed were Poland (nearly 91 percent), Greece (86 percent), Lithuania (85 percent), and Slovakia (nearly 80 percent). Those nations with large Slavic populations had especially rough treatment by the Germans. Other areas were in a better position to help. Unoccupied France (Vichy) was more willing to help French Jews than refugees from other countries. Italy protected its Jews until the Germans moved in as conquerors rather than as partners in 1943. Even then, many Italian Jews were hidden away, and only 17 percent were sent to concentration camps.

DENMARK kept its democratic government and popular king, Christian X. At the Wannsee Conference, it was decided that pushing Denmark to send its Jews to the death camps should be delayed. It was not until 1943 that the word was leaked that Danish Jews were to be arrested. A network of aid developed within days. Jews were hidden away until fishing boats could take them across the Baltic to Sweden. Danes contributed to pay the expense of transporting poor Jews. Of Denmark's Jews, only 400 were taken, and they were sent to Theresienstadt; the Danish government and people kept a close eye on them, and only 51 died, all of natural causes.

FINLAND had a small Jewish population, which was protected by Prime Minister Johann Rangel. When pressed by Himmler to cooperate with the Final Solution, the Finns told them they "had no Jewish problem." Only seven refugee Jews were turned over to the Germans. To protect their Jews, the Finns sent them to safety in Sweden.

The Final Solution failed to achieve its goal partly because of the righteous who refused to surrender Jews to it.

ACTIVITY:

Going through the steps before a person will help someone in trouble, have the class decide why some people try to stop a fight on the playground while others only stand around and watch. Then have them consider the risks of taking in Jews, and ask whether they would have wanted to do it.

Name _____ Date _____

Challenges

1. Why might the hider's family urge him or her to stop hiding Jews? _____

_____

2. Why did the Italian policeman tell the Jews he was going to arrest them the next morning?

_____

3. What Swedish diplomat was especially helpful to Jews? _____

4. How did the Swedish diplomat help? _____

_____

_____

5. Who financed Schindler's factory at Krakow? _____

_____

6. How many did Schindler save from the gas chambers? _____

7. What French Protestant community saved thousands of Jews? _____

8. What did Zegota do to help Jews in Poland? _____

_____

_____

9. The Jews from what three nations suffered the greatest percentage of deaths during the Holocaust? _____

10. What country discussed gave the least number of Jews to the Nazis? _____

Points to Consider

1. What kinds of reasons might a person have who decided to protect or hide Jews?
2. The Huguenots had been persecuted themselves and had suffered a terrible massacre in 1572 (St. Bartholomew's Day Massacre). Do you think that might have affected their attitude toward the Holocaust?
3. What conditions made it easier for Denmark and Finland to save more Jews than it would have been possible to save in Poland and Western Russia?

The End of the Camps

The camp at Birkenau as it appears today.

In 1944, the signs were on the wall; Germany was losing the war on every front. Allied bombers flew over German cities with little or no opposition from the once mighty *Luftwaffe.* The invasion at Normandy was followed by a Russian advance on the Eastern Front. From Himmler to the lowly SS guard at a concentration camp, the possibility that their actions were soon going to be visible to the Allies was a scary thought indeed.

Hitler became even more determined to finish the destruction of Jews. In his twisted mind, the international Jewish conspiracy had brought this destruction on the Third Reich, and now the Jews must suffer. Like the Babylonian king centuries before, he would heat up the furnace seven times hotter than ever before (Daniel 4:16-23). The trains *must* reach the death camps, and the Jews *must* all be killed.

Hitler's only consolation during the last year of the war were reports that Jews were being killed faster than ever. The Warsaw underground informed London that 13 trains a day were arriving at Auschwitz with 40 to 50 cars per train. The Jews on the train believed they were being exchanged for German POWs or were being resettled in the east. Not until the train pulled into the station did they realize the danger they were in.

Jews in the camp became more defiant. Even those on their way to be gassed were speaking up. One woman about to die stepped out of line and warned the SS guards the world knew what was going on here, and they were going to pay dearly for it.

ATTEMPTED DEALS. Some Nazi leaders were feeling the heat, and wanted to trade Jews for supplies. Joel Brand, a Zionist and German refugee, met with Adolf Eichmann, the Nazi "expert on Jewish affairs;" the Nazi offered to trade one million Jewish lives for 10,000 trucks, coffee, sugar, tea, and soap. The trucks were only to be used on the Russian front. The United States and England turned the deal down quickly, sure that the motive was to split Allied unity. A week after the Normandy invasion, the Germans offered to trade 30,000 Jews for 20 million Swiss francs.

PLAYING WITH NUMBERS. In August 1944, Eichmann reported to Himmler that six million Jews had been killed. Two-thirds of those had died in camps, and the others had been killed by mobile units. Himmler wanted the figure to be higher, and he sent a statistical expert to look at the records. In November, Hitler considered the Final Solution completed and ordered that the death camps be destroyed. After meeting with Himmler, Auschwitz's commandant Hoess asked SS officers to destroy the Birkenau camp and told them to remove all traces of persons, barracks, gas chambers, and crematoria quickly.

SHUFFLING PRISONERS. With Allied troops closing in, a mad scramble began as camp officials began sending prisoners to camps farther into the interior. Some were sent by trains, others by forced marches. Those unable to keep up were shot; many died of hunger or exhaustion, or froze to death. One group of women at the Hindenburg camp were given some dry bread and boarded on open cars. The first camp they were sent to was too full, so they were moved to Bergen-Belsen. On their long journey, they were given no water and used snow to slake their thirst. Near Dachau, American troops found freight cars with 2,000 bodies in them. They had been left to suffocate, starve, or die of exposure.

Other prisoners were murdered where they were. At Gleiwitz, 57 prisoners in the hospital were locked up, and the building was set on fire. Those attempting to escape were shot. Incredibly, two prisoners escaped by hiding under the corpses.

THE END. As Allied troops reached a few miles from the camps, many guards deserted, dressed themselves as civilians, and blended in with the general population. It was their turn to live in fear.

Liberation. The Nazi efforts to destroy the evidence of their crimes failed. Some crematoria still stood. Many records were destroyed, but too many survived. The distorted bodies of victims remained unburned. Huge piles of eyeglasses, shoes, and hair were left behind. Even worse for the Nazis, many of their starved victims were still alive to testify against them.

REACTIONS. Russian General Vasily Petrenko, a battle-hardened soldier, found the horror of Auschwitz beyond description. The thing that troubled him most was what the Nazis had done to children. He said: "How did they find themselves there? I just couldn't digest it." U.S. General Eisenhower toured Ohrdruf camp with Generals Bradley and Patton. Eisenhower saw the whole camp because he wanted to testify in case someone denied it had happened. He described the experience as "overpowering." Bradley said: "The smell of death overwhelmed us," and Patton threw up.

At Buchenwald, Patton was outraged that prisoners starved while civilians outside the fence were well fed. He sent MPs to round up 1,000 citizens of nearby Weimar to see what the Nazis had done. The MPs brought 2,000 instead. They were shocked, and some fainted.

INMATE REACTION. Many inmates were too weak to say or do much. Some shouted in their native languages, "Viva Amerikaniski." They tried to clap, but they had so little skin on their hands that it did not sound like clapping. Many reached out to touch their liberators. In their starved condition, the inmates were desperate for food. Some GIs innocently offered them the only food they had—candy bars. It killed the inmates whose stomachs were too shriveled up for regular food. After that, the army sent nutrition experts to provide the right foods to restore their bodies.

INTERNATIONAL REACTION. Newsreels showed the world what had happened, and people realized this was far beyond the bounds of suffering that was normal in war. This was murder, and those responsible were to answer for what they had done.

ACTIVITY:

Camp inmates who had been held for a long time were going to have trouble adjusting to a normal life again. Have the class make a list of things inmates needed to adjust to before they were ready to leave the camp.

Name _____ Date _____

Challenges

1. What were three signs that the end was near for the Nazis in 1944? _____

_____

_____

2. What was Hitler's reaction to the incoming bad news? _____

_____

3. What did Eichmann want in return for saving a million Jewish lives? _____

_____

4. Why did the Americans and British turn down the offer? _____

_____

5. What did Himmler and Hoess want done at Birkenau? _____

_____

6. According to Eichmann's figures, how many Jews had been killed in the camps? _____

_____

7. What was some of the evidence the Nazis failed to destroy? _____

_____

8. What bothered General Petrenko the most about Auschwitz? _____

_____

9. What part of the experience seemed to bother General Bradley the most? _____

_____

10. What was the German civilians' reaction when they were taken to Buchenwald? _____

_____

Points to Consider

1. Does it appear that Hitler and Himmler were in agreement on what to do about Jews in late 1944 and 1945? Why?

2. If you were a concentration camp guard caught by the Allies, how would you answer questions about why you had been part of that operation?

3. An inmate told American journalist Edward R. Murrow: "To write about this, you must have been here at least two years…and after that, you don't want to write any more." What do you think he meant by that statement?

The Day of Judgment: Nuremberg

Jeremiah had told his people in an earlier time that they would suffer hard times, but then "all who devour you shall be devoured, and all your foes…shall be slaves." Nazi leaders were now the ones fearful of being devoured as manhunts began for those responsible. At the camps, some guards were caught, and inmates pointed out those who had been decent and those who had been cruel. Despite orders requiring that the guards be held for trial, some Allied soldiers turned them over to the inmates or reported them "shot while trying to escape." But these were the minnows, and it was the sharks who became the major focus of attention.

Justice required that the inmates who had died in such horrible ways be given decent burial. Chaplains performed gravesite religious ceremonies with great dignity.

An officer of the Waffen-SS is captured by an Allied soldier.

THE SUICIDES. Some Nazi leaders killed themselves before they could be brought to trial. Hitler killed himself as Berlin was falling, on May 1, 1945. After giving poison to his wife and six children, Goebbels wrote his Final Testament expressing his devotion to Hitler, then took poison. Himmler disguised himself as an SS enlisted man, but he was recognized and taken prisoner. During a physical exam, Himmler bit down on a vial of poison hidden between his teeth. No grave markers stand for any of them.

TRIALS. One by one, most Nazi leaders were captured within a short time. Stalin would have preferred killing them without a trial, but the United States and England demanded and got a formal trial. The location selected was Nuremberg, the city where the great Nazi rallies had been held. The trials lasted from November 1945 to October 1946. The presiding judge was British Lord Justice Geoffrey Lawrence; other judges were Francis Biddle (U.S.), Henri Donnedieu (Fr.), and General I.T. Nikitchenko (U.S.S.R.). Prosecutors included Robert Jackson of the U.S. Supreme Court. Defendants picked defense attorneys from a list provided for them by the judges.

The crimes of which they were accused fell into four categories: (1) conspiracy to commit crimes in other categories, (2) crimes against peace, (3) war crimes, and (4) crimes against humanity. The high-profile defendants were Hermann Goering, Rudolf Hess, General Alfred Jodl, Albert Speer, and Admiral Karl Doenitz, German chancellor for the week after Hitler's death.

In his opening statement at the trial, Jackson told the judges: "History does not record a crime perpetrated against so many victims or ever carried out with such calculated cruelty." In his summary before the court on July 26, 1946, he said: "If you were to say of these men that they are not guilty, it would be true to say there has been no war, there have been no slain, there has been no crime."

The testimony and documents filled volumes. While the trials covered a number of topics, responsibility for the Holocaust provided some of the most gripping evidence. For example, a remark was noted in the diary of Poland's Nazi governor, Hans Frank, regarding conditions in the Warsaw ghetto: "Just a marginal remark—we have condemned a million and a half Jews to death by starvation." Witness after witness, document after document, and diary entries one after another all told the story of brutal executions and horrible conditions inside concentration camps.

Of the 22 defendants, only three were released. Twelve were sentenced to death, three to life in prison, and the rest to prison terms of 10 to 20 years. Goering, sentenced to death by hanging, killed himself with poison.

These famous defendants were only a few of those involved, and others were later tried by different courts. The most famous of these trials was at Frankfurt from December 1963 to August 1965, where the defendants were officers and doctors at Auschwitz. By that time, enthusiasm for punishing Nazis had declined so much that six received life in prison, three were released, and the other 12 received sentences from three years and six months to 14 years of hard labor.

Trials were also held for those directly responsible for carrying out Nazi policies. One was Otto Ohlendorf, SS general for the Ukraine, who never showed concern for victims, but only looked for cheaper and easier ways of killing Jews. Sentenced in 1948, he was executed in 1951.

Of concentration camp supervisors tried, two examples give the picture. Josef Kramer, the "beast of Belsen," regretted nothing he had done. After his capture, he took British officers on a tour of the prison and walked past rats and corpses without expressing any remorse or regret. When questioned about gassing women prisoners, he said: "I had no feeling in carrying out those things because I had received an order." He was tried by a British court and sentenced to death in November 1945.

Irma Grese, called the "blond Angel of Death" at Auschwitz, had found great pleasure in whipping women prisoners and watching painful operations being performed on them. Sentenced to death, she had to be dragged to the gallows.

Some war criminals escaped. Adolf Eichmann, responsible for so much of Hitler's Final Solution, went to Argentina where he was captured by the Israelis in 1961 and was executed by them in 1962. Dr. Josef Mengele, the doctor who had conducted cruel experiments at Auschwitz, escaped to South America and lived in hiding until his death. Heinrich Muller, an important Gestapo chief, reportedly died when the Russians captured Berlin; rumors spread he was still alive and living in Argentina, and he was put on the list of most-wanted Nazis in 1973. Martin Bormann, Hitler's right-hand man, was never found.

The trials, with testimony and documents presented, preserved a record of the dark world the Nazis created, one without justice, mercy, or sympathy. The defendant's excuse was constantly repeated: "I was only following orders."

ACTIVITY:

Have the class debate whether a person should be let off because he or she was only following orders.

Name _____ Date _____

Challenges

1. What was done for the victims? _____

_____

2. How did Goebbels die? _____

_____

3. How did Himmler try to disguise himself? _____

_____

4. Who were two Americans involved in the Nuremberg trials? _____

_____

5. Which of the categories of crimes do you think was most likely to be involved with the Holocaust?

_____

6. How many Jews did Hans Frank write had been condemned to death by starvation?

_____

7. How many Nuremberg defendants were put to death? _____

_____

8. Why did Josef Kramer say he felt no regret in what he had done? _____

_____

9. Where did Eichmann go to avoid capture? Who caught him? _____

_____

10. What happened to Bormann? _____

_____

Points to Consider

1. What was the advantage in trying the defendants rather than just taking them out to be shot?
2. Do you think the indifferent attitudes of the defendants would have made you vote for their execution?
3. Do you think it was fair to try people for crimes when, in their nation, the things they did were not crimes?

Zionism Fulfilled: The Birth of Israel

In the nineteenth century, the concept of Zionism was born. Its message was that Jews were never going to be accepted in Europe, so Jews should create their own nation. The leader of the movement, Theodor Herzl, faced some perplexing questions: Where would this nation be located, was it to be religious or secular, and would Zionism lead to new anti-Semitism? Zionism was more popular in Eastern Europe where Jews tried to keep a separate identity. In Western Europe, Jews were more interested in fitting into the broader society. The Nazi era caused Zionism to be taken much more seriously by many Jews.

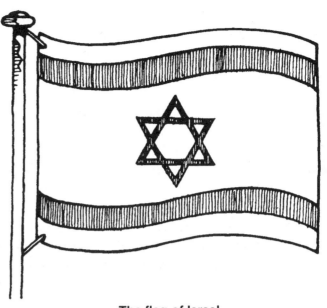

The flag of Israel

Despite Hitler's goal of wiping out all Jews in Europe and Himmler's belief that the Final Solution had achieved its goal, about five million Jews had survived. Many of these were barely alive in the camps and needed much medical care before they could go out into the world again. For them, the stress of brutal treatment was replaced by a growing concern for their future. If they were from Eastern Europe, they had reason to worry. Their homes and perhaps their town had disappeared, and family and friends were probably dead. Their Gentile neighbors did not like them before; why would they like them any better now?

For the time being, there was the need for medical care. They were frail and diseased, and many died within weeks of being liberated. As health returned, anxiety increased; what was to happen to them now? The Allied authorities decided that a person who had been born a Pole, Russian, Dutch, etc., must return to the land of their birth, even if they did not want to go, and even if they would not be safe. When DPs (displaced persons) heard of the policy, there were pitiful scenes. A Jewish soldier loading DPs on a truck bound for Poland was told by one man: "You might as well kill me now. I am dead anyway if I go to Poland."

The Jews had good reason to be afraid. A tragic example occurred at Kielce, Poland, which had a large Jewish community before the war. When the war ended, only 150 Kielce Jews returned. The ancient accusation that Jews killed children and drank their blood aroused mob action, and a riot followed. As in the pogroms of Russia, the police stepped in, but only to take weapons from the Jews. By the end of the riot, 42 Jews were killed and 50 injured. Clearly, the Jews needed another place to go.

Many would have preferred to go to America, but the United States accepted only 200,000 over four years, and a mountain of paperwork faced them. Many other countries were even less welcoming. Zionism was stronger than before.

PALESTINE had been under British control since World War I. In 1917, England adopted the *Balfour Declaration*, which read: "His Majesty's government view with favour the establishment in Palestine of a national home for the Jewish people…it being clearly understood that nothing shall be done which may prejudice the civil and religious rights of existing non-Jewish communities in Palestine…." How to create a Jewish state without prejudicing the rights of Arabs was a mystery.

From 1919 to 1933, the Jewish population in Palestine increased from 65,000 to 200,000. In the first three years of Nazi rule in Germany, many more Jews went to Palestine. The more Jews who came, the louder the Arabs protested. In 1939, British Colonial Secretary Malcolm MacDonald issued the *White Paper*. It would create an independent nation in Palestine, with power shared between Arabs and Jews according to their numbers. Over the next five years, 75,000 Jews could immigrate to Palestine; after that, the number entering was to be worked out with the Arabs. Most of Palestine, however, was to be closed to Jewish settlers.

The British expected a flood of Jews to come to Palestine after the war, and they wanted to stop the flow. The Jews in Palestine were determined to increase the numbers coming. Guerilla warfare between Jews and Arabs made Palestine nearly impossible to control.

In the Jewish-Arab struggle, the Jews had the advantage. About 30,000 had served in the British Brigade during the war and had returned with their weapons and training. The oldest Jewish organization involved was the *Haganah*, which mostly fought Arabs. Two other groups, the *Irgun* (National Military Organization) and the *Stern Group*, led by Monachem Begin (who later served as Israel's prime minister), often battled the British. The British made every effort to keep Palestine under control, but their efforts were in vain. They tried curfews, lightning raids, and sweeps of neighborhoods. Weapons and rebels were found, but that did not prevent more violence against British troops. Tired of it all, the British turned the issue over to the United Nations in 1947.

ISRAEL. The United States was growing anxious about solving this problem. Many DPs were in the American sector of Germany, and the cost of caring for them irritated American taxpayers. President Truman was sympathetic to the victims of the camps and pushed for the creation of a State of Israel. On May 14, 1948, Israel announced its independence, and the United States recognized it a few minutes later. Israel was soon attacked by its Arab neighbors, but it quickly defeated them. In 1949, a truce was arranged by an American diplomat, Dr. Ralph Bunche.

In a personal letter to Israel's president, Dr. Chaim Weizmann, President Truman wrote on November 29, 1948: "I want to tell you how happy and impressed I have been at the remarkable progress of the new State of Israel. What you have received at the hands of the world has been far less than was your due. But you have more than made the most of what you have received, and I admire you for it."

Israel has achieved remarkable success over the years. But in spite of its concern for the future, it has never forgotten the tragedy suffered by the Jews during the Holocaust.

ACTIVITY:

Have the class look up information on the State of Israel to learn more about its people, its geography, and its troubles with its Arab neighbors.

Name _____ Date _____

Challenges

1. Who was the major leader in early Zionism? _____

2. How many European Jews survived the Holocaust? _____

3. Where did Jews and other refugees have to go after the war? _____

_____

4. What does DP stand for? _____

5. What happened when Jews returned to Kielce? _____

_____

_____

6. What document called for establishing a national homeland for Jews? _____

_____

7. The *White Paper* allowed only how many Jews to move to Palestine in the next five years?

_____

8. Who did the *Haganah* fight most of the time? _____

_____

9. Who was the U.S. president when Israel became independent? _____

_____

10. When did Israel become independent? _____

Points to Consider

1. Do you think it was fair for people to have to return to the nation of their birth? Why do you think the Allies made that decision?

2. As a Jew, how would you have interpreted the *Balfour Declaration* if you had been alive in 1917? How would you have interpreted it as an Arab?

3. As an Israeli today, how might the events of the late 1940s make you feel about England and the United States today?

Could the Holocaust Have Been Avoided?

One of the most disturbing questions about the Holocaust is whether it was avoidable, or whether it at least could have been limited. Nations take care of their own people first, so helping others seems less important to them. In the early 1930s during the Great Depression, Europe and the United States reeled from unemployment, soup kitchens, and bread lines, and they wondered if life would ever improve. The last thing they wanted was a new group of hungry people to feed. With the situation bleak everywhere, immigration declined because people felt they could go hungry at home more easily than in a strange country. In 1929, 46,000 Germans immigrated to the U.S.; only 1,919 came in 1933. By 1937, German immigration was over 10,000 again, and was 33,000 in 1939. There

A Star of David badge like those German Jews were forced to wear during the Nazi era

were, of course, other places German Jews could go, but "No Immigrants Welcome" signs were up everywhere. Unfortunately, the Jews who did escape Germany often fled to countries soon to be overrun.

The responsibility for the Holocaust clearly falls on Hitler. His aim was clear from the first page of *Mein Kampf* to the death of his last victim in a death camp. No outsider could have persuaded him to change course. However, the outside world could have done more.

EUROPEAN DEMOCRACIES could have stopped Hitler in his tracks if they had not tried appeasement (giving in to demands). Anti-Semitism was strong in both England and France. Neither country made the *Kristallnacht* a major issue; it was Hitler's land-grabbing—not his cruel treatment of Jews—that moved them to action.

THE ROLE OF THE UNITED STATES. During the *Anschluss,* thousands of Austrian Jews lined up outside foreign embassies, hoping for visas to enter other countries, but the paperwork moved as slowly as ever. President Roosevelt called an international conference that met at Evian, France. Representatives from 32 countries and 20 Jewish and 19 non-Jewish refugee agencies met and talked about the urgent need to help Jews resettle. The Dominican Republic offered to take 500; no one else offered to take any more than their usual immigration quotas. Hitler knew now that no one wanted his Jews.

After *Kristallnacht,* Roosevelt allowed the 15,000 Germans and Austrians with visitor status to remain in the United States, but he did nothing more. The world should have known that intense pressure was being put on German Jews, but except for official protests and threats of boycotts against German-made goods, the attitude was generally indifferent. An example of that was the voyage of the ship *St. Louis,* which sailed from Hamburg in May 1939 with 900 German Jews on board. They had purchased entry permits from Cuba and hoped to eventually be allowed to enter the United States. When the ship arrived in Havana, the Cuban government refused to let them in, so the ship had to move on. Everywhere the *St. Louis* went, the passengers were rejected. Jewish organizations raised money and finally persuaded England, Holland, Belgium, and France to divide the refugees among them.

Anti-Semitism and opposition to allowing more immigrants to enter the United States combined to keep them from coming. A Gallup poll showed that 80 percent of Americans opposed changing immigration laws.

In August 1943, a Polish diplomat, Jan Karski, met with Roosevelt. He told the president about death camps in Poland. He wanted the United States to bomb railroads, gas chambers, and crematoria, but nothing was done. Part of the reason was that the State Department found a problem in every approach to helping Jews. The official handling refugee questions, Assistant Secretary of State Breckinridge Long, said Communists and even Nazis might be smuggled in among any group of refugees. Secretary of State Hull told the president: "The unknown cost of removing an undetermined number of persons from an undisclosed place to an unknown destination…is out of the question."

A Treasury Department lawyer discovered that the State Department was hiding information about the Holocaust from the president and trying to cut off any new reports on the subject. Secretary of the Treasury Morgenthau talked to Roosevelt about the evidence in January 1944, and the president set up the War Refugee Board a few days later. It helped after the war ended, but it was of little use in saving millions of lives during the war.

The suggestion that bombs be dropped on rail connections and gas chambers ran into opposition as well. In December 1942, the Polish resistance sent reports about the genocide (deliberate murder of a large group) of Jews. Their report was confirmed by the OSS (forerunner of the CIA). The Poles urged that railroads, gas chambers, and crematoria be bombed. The U.S. military refused because it would divert aircraft from bombing military targets, and they thought the best way to help concentration camp inmates was quick victory in the war.

The difficulties of reaching targets in Poland in 1942 had been solved by 1944. Despite pleas from the World Jewish Congress, bombing was always postponed. Assistant Secretary of War John McCloy wrote in August 1944 that such an attack would require great air support, and even if it were practical, it "might provoke even more vindictive action by the Germans."

That same month, American bombers with fighter escorts flew over the railway to Auschwitz and bombed the synthetic rubber factory at Buna, five miles away. No bombs came near Auschwitz or its rail connections.

Churchill found the same reluctance by his military to act. The Royal Air Force and Foreign Office always found excuses not to act. The Foreign Office was more concerned about relations with Arab oil producers than the inmates of the camps. When the possibility of sending Hungarian Jews to Palestine was suggested, a British official asked: "What shall I do with a million Jews? Where shall I put them?"

The responsibility for the tragedy of the Holocaust remains with Hitler and his Nazi henchmen, but the harm they brought to millions could have been reduced before and during the war. Prejudice is a disease that not only affects the mind, but the heart, eyes, and ears as well.

ACTIVITY:

Have the class debate whether the United States and England could have done more to prevent the Holocaust. If they decide they could have, ask what they could have done. If they decide they could not have, ask the reasons why it was difficult or impossible.

Name _____ Date _____

Challenges

1. What caused the drop in German immigration to the United States between 1929 and 1933?

_____

2. What is appeasement? _____

3. What international conference discussed the Jewish problem in 1938? _____

_____

4. Who were the passengers on the *St. Louis,* and to what country were they going? _____

_____

5. What happened when they got to Havana? _____

_____

6. How did Americans feel about changing immigration laws? _____

_____

7. What reason did Assistant Secretary Long give for opposing the transport of Jews to America?

_____

8. Who told Roosevelt that information was being hidden from him? _____

_____

9. What did the Polish resistance want the United States to do? _____

_____

10. What group did the British Foreign Office not want to offend? _____

_____

Points to Consider

1. Do you think people opposing immigration are all prejudiced against those wanting to enter the country? Why?

2. If you were Hitler and saw the results of the Evian Conference, what would you conclude about anti-Semitism in Europe and the United States?

3. If you were a Jewish bomber pilot, what concerns would you have had if you had been ordered to destroy the crematoria at Auschwitz?

Lessons From the Holocaust

Many in Germany and German-occupied countries were content to let the Nazis harass and destroy "inferior" peoples as long as they themselves were not bothered. However, they failed to realize that unless the Nazis were stopped, they would continue to label anyone they chose as "inferior" or "subhuman" and target more and more groups for destruction.

1. FREE LUNCHES. There is an old saying that "There's no such thing as a free lunch." Every action has its price. To make an "A" in a course may require missing a party, so the student has to decide which is more important: the "A" or the party. In desperate situations, the student might be more concerned with survival than principles. Students may cheat on a test because that is the only way they can make the honor roll. They will hate themselves tomorrow, but today, it's the grade that counts.

This "free lunch" principle affects nations as well as individuals. In the early 1930s, the Great Depression affected most of the world. Unemployment in the United States reached 24.9 percent in 1932; in Germany, it was over 50 percent. Desperate people look to anyone who can rescue them, even if their solutions make no sense or would be considered immoral in normal times. Leaders like Hitler and Stalin offered cures for their nation's problems. The medicine was strong, and the price looked cheap. Hitler told Germans: "Lift up your heads; be proud to be Germans. There are devils among us: Communists, liberals, Jews, Gypsies. When these devils are destroyed, your misery will be destroyed." He claimed Germany's problems were caused by outsiders, and the blame was with the Treaty of Versailles, international Jewish bankers, and German Jews, who were not German at all, but visitors who had outworn their welcome. Germans cheered, raised their right arms, and said "Sieg Heil!"

Hitler was offering a free lunch. The people were tired of street demonstrations, so he arrested Communists and even his own SA, who helped him rise to power. His secret police and SS restored order at the price of civil liberties. People wanted jobs, so he started building projects, including lavish government buildings and *autobahns* (super highways). But who paid for them? The Jews were charged high taxes for the privilege of leaving Germany, and they were taxed heavily if they stayed. German glory was being built at the Jews' expense. It was a glory also paid for by conquered peoples, not the German public. German taxpayers liked that.

In the end, however, Germany paid dearly, with a war, mass destruction, loss of property, thousands of lives, and loss of self-respect. Hitler, Himmler, and many of the Nazi leaders lost their lives. There is always a price.

The world paid a price for its indifference as well. Jews were a major part of Europe's intellectual life: doctors, lawyers, and scientists. Many Gentiles resented their success, but they forgot the reason they had succeeded was hard work. The less successful, lazy, and incompetent often envy the success of the hard worker. However, if you lose the person who uses his or her brain, you lose progress.

2. POWER. Put too much power in anyone's hand, and it leads to disaster. Lord Acton's famous comment that: "Power corrupts and absolute power corrupts absolutely" was certainly true in the Nazi era. Everyone from Goering stealing Jewish-owned art treasures to SS guards blackmailing concentration camp inmates or pocketing some of the loot to be found in the "Canadas" was corrupted. Every guard with a whip in his hand had unlimited power over inmates.

This abuse of power spread beyond the camps. Any land or property in occupied Europe was available to any German official who wanted it. Hitler planned to take all worthwhile farm land in occupied Poland and Russia and give it to German farmers. The skilled workers among the Jews, Czechs, Poles, and others would provide slave labor for German industries. The Jews were among the first victims, but eventually, others were going to be included in the list of those suffering.

In the end, Hitler's obsession with power destroyed him and his dream. His dream of glory led him to war with the two nations he most feared and respected: Great Britain and the United States.

3. APATHY TOWARD EVIL. Each of us has a tendency to ignore abuses as long as they don't affect us. We might watch a dictator murdering thousands in his own country, and say: "I'm glad I don't live there." But problems in Country A tend to spread to its neighbor, Country B, because dictators often stir up trouble with other nations to justify requiring strict obedience from their own people. The expansion of Germany, Italy, and Japan in the 1930s gives evidence of what can happen.

Martin Niemoller may have said it best. He supported Hitler when he came to power, but by 1935, he had seen what Nazism stood for and attacked it from the pulpit. He was arrested and ended up in solitary confinement at Dachau. After the war, he made a famous statement: "First, they came after the socialists, and I did not speak out—because I was not a socialist. Then they came for the trade unionists, and I did not speak out—because I was not a trade unionist. Then they came for the Jews, and I did not speak out—because I was not a Jew. Then they came for me—and there was no one left to speak for me."

When any person or any group is picked on, and they have done nothing to provoke the attack, the time for protest comes before they come to pick on you.

4. PREJUDICE is a terrible beast to let loose on the world, and if it is allowed to roam free, it brings out the worst in human nature. Look at what happened in Germany. It began with defining who was a Jew, and that led to humiliation, suffering, and death for millions. It is good to be proud of your school, team, city, state, and nation, and you should do everything possible to make them better. But to wish evil on someone else, to assume they are hardly worthy of living, does not make you better. Germany learned that lesson the hard way. In time, they suffered for those years when Prejudice had ruled their land.

Name _____ Date _____

Vocabulary

Below are certain terms that have been used to describe attitudes that led to or supported the Holocaust. For each one, (1) look in a dictionary for its definition, (2) apply it to the Holocaust, and (3) think of a modern example where you think it might apply.

1. **Prejudice:** _____

_____

_____

_____

2. **Discrimination:** _____

_____

_____

_____

3. **Racism:** _____

_____

_____

_____

4. **Persecution:** _____

_____

_____

_____

5. **Apathy:** _____

_____

_____

_____

6. **Genocide:** _____

_____

_____

_____

Quotes to Consider

Much has been written about the Holocaust. The following are some quotes from people involved, either as the persecutor or the victim. Read them and discuss their meaning.

Adolf Hitler in *Mein Kampf.* "He [the Jew] contaminates art, literature, the theater, makes a mockery of natural feeling, overthrows all concepts of beauty, of the noble and the good, and instead drags men down into the sphere of his own base nature."

Excerpts from Editor's Law 1933. "The position of editor-in-chief is a public task, of which the professional duties and rights are regulated by the State through this law.... Only those persons can be editors who…are of Aryan descent, and are not married to a person of non-Aryan descent."

Excerpt from the Citizenship Law 1935. "A Jew cannot be a citizen of the Reich. He has no right to vote in public affairs and he cannot occupy public office. Jewish officials will retire as of 31 December 1935. If these officials served at the front in the world war, either for Germany or her allies, they will receive in full, until they reach the age limit, the pension to which they were entitled according to the salary they last received; they will, however, not advance in seniority."

American Consul David Buffum reporting on *Kristallnacht* in Leipzig, 1938. "The shattering of shop windows, looting of stores and dwellings of Jews which began in the early hours of 10 November 1938, was hailed…in the Nazi press as a 'spontaneous wave of righteous indignation throughout Germany.... So far as a very high percentage of the German populace is concerned, a state of popular indignation that would lead to such excesses can be considered as nonexistent.

The most hideous phase of the so-called 'spontaneous' action has been the wholesale arrest and transportation to concentration camps of male German Jews between the ages of sixteen and sixty.... The insatiably sadistic perpetrators threw many of the trembling inmates into a small stream that flows through the Zoological Park, commanding horrified spectators to spit at them, defile them with mud, and jeer at their plight. The latter incident has been repeatedly corroborated by German witnesses who were nauseated in telling the tale."

Anne Frank, *Diary of a Young Girl,* June 20, 1942. "After May 1940 the good times were few and far between: first there was the war, then the capitulation, and then the arrival of the Germans, which is when trouble started for the Jews. Our freedom was severely restricted by a series of anti-Jewish decrees: Jews were required to wear a yellow star; Jews were required to turn in their bicycles; Jews were forbidden to use street cars; Jews were forbidden to ride in cars, even their own; Jews were required to do their shopping between 3 and 5 p.m.... Jews were forbidden to attend theaters, movies, or any other form of entertainment…. You couldn't do this and you couldn't do that, but life went on. Jacque always said to me, 'I don't dare do anything anymore, cause I'm afraid it's not allowed.'"

Martin Niemoller, longtime inmate of Dachau. "First they came for the socialists, and I did not speak out—because I was not a socialist. Then they came for the trade unionists, and I did not speak out—because I was not a trade unionist. Then they came for the Jews, and I did not speak out—because I was not a Jew. Then they came for me—and there was no one left to speak for me."

<u>Primo Levi</u>, *Survival At Auschwitz.* "Experience had shown us many times the vanity of every conjecture: why worry oneself trying to read into the future when no action, no word of ours could have the minimum influence."

<u>Elie Wiesel</u> in *Night,* discussing his first 24 hours at Auschwitz. "Toward five o'clock in the morning, we were driven out of the barracks. The Kapos beat us once more, but I had ceased to feel any pain from their blows. An icy wind enveloped us. We were naked, our shoes and belts in our hands. The command: 'Run!' And we ran. After a few minutes of racing, a new barracks. A barrel of petrol at the entrance. Disinfection. Everyone was soaked in it. Then a hot shower. At high speed. As we came out from the water, we were driven outside. More running. Another barracks, the store. Very long tables. Mountains of prison clothes. On we ran. As we passed, trousers, tunic, shirt, and socks were thrown to us. Within a few seconds, we had ceased to be men."

[After witnessing the execution of a small boy] "Behind me, I heard the same man asking: 'Where is God now?' And I heard a voice within me answer him: 'Where is He? Here He is—He is hanging here on the gallows.'"

<u>Marching song</u> of slave labor brigades of the Libau ghetto:
"We are the ghetto Jews, the loneliest people on earth.
Everything we had we lost, we have nothing left of worth."

<u>Adolf Eichmann</u> at his trial for crimes against humanity. "To be frank with you, had we killed all of them, the 10.3 million, I would be happy and say, 'Alright, we managed to destroy an enemy.'"

Challenge Answers

The Roots of Anti-Semitism (page 6)
1. Councils ordered Jews to wear special yellow badges, and live separated from Gentiles.
2. Marranos: Spanish Jews who converted to Catholicism
3. King Edward I; Oliver Cromwell
4. Colony: Rhode Island
5. Napoleon told them to become part of French civilization.
6. Maria Theresa: Unbearded Jewish men were required to wear a yellow badge; Jews could not shop until after 9:00 for vegetables or for cattle before 11:00.
7. Pogroms were times when Jews and their property could be attacked without punishment.
8. Pogroms were used to relieve public tension.
9. Mendellsohn translated the Torah into German.
10. Anti-Semites brought up old charges against the Jews.

Years of Turmoil in Germany (page 9)
1. Europe was very enthusiastic.
2. Russians picked on Jewish villages in the Pale.
3. Armenians were Christians in Turkey. Many were killed.
4. The Treaty took away the German air force and navy and reduced the army to 100,000.
5. Germany was forced to sign; it said Germany was responsible for the war.
6. Sparticists were Communists; their leaders were killed.
7. Inflation: 4.2 billion marks per $1
8. German Worker's Party
9. Symbol: swastika; greeting: Heil!
10. SA were recognized by their brown shirts.

The Nazi Rise to Power (page 12)
1. Outsiders: the French, international Jewish conspiracy, and Communists.
2. *Volk:* national race, The *Führer* (leader)
3. The Nationalist party was more respectable and had ties to business leaders.
4. Communists and Socialists
5. Von Papen: He expected to be vice chancellor and his friends would hold high offices.
6. Goering stole art for his collection.
7. Himmler rented concentration camp inmates to be slave labor for big businesses.
8. Josef Goebbels; repeated lies over and over
9. Gestapo: political police
10. Roehm was shot.

The Nazi View of Religion and Race (page 15)
1. Jesus taught that only God should be feared; Hitler wanted the people to fear him.
2. Mission: create a world free from Jews and other "subhumans"
3. The Catholic church promised to stay out of German politics.
4. The Pope accused Hitler of violating the Concordat of 1933.
5. Leader: Martin Neimoller; He was put in Dachau.
6. Faith Movement: Jesus was Aryan, not Jewish.
7. Eugenics: an effort in science to create perfect humans
8. Eliminate those who were defective.
9. Teaching children to think
10. Himmler started *Lebensborn* and kidnapped Polish children who had Aryan qualities.

The Nazi Attack on German Jews Begins (page 18)
1. Subjects
2. Mongrel or mixed breed
3. An SA or SS "defensive guard"
4. The Reich Citizenship Law took away the right to vote or hold public office.
5. Berlin Olympics
6. About 90 percent favored uniting with Germany.
7. Mauthausen
8. The killing of vom Rath
9. Night of the Broken Glass
10. 402,000 left; the United States accepted only 27,000 German immigrants a year.

The Drive to the East *(Drang Nach Osten)* (page 21)
1. Jewish market towns
2. Region of eastern Poland with large Jewish population
3. German Jews looked down on them.
4. Nara
5. Took their property and sent Jews to labor camps where many died

6. They were treated so badly by the Russians.

7. Germany attacked Poland.

9. Jewish councils set up to run ghettos

9. Had rocks thrown at them by people dressed as Poles

10. 2,613 calories for Germans; 669 for Poles; 184 for Jews

Hitler Attacks Western Europe (page 24)

1. Sitzkrieg and phony war
2. France
3. Danes were pure Aryans and surrendered without a fight.
4. Bankers stalled long enough for Jews to withdraw their money.
5. 25,000
6. They joined hands and jumped to their deaths.
7. Seyss-Inquart and Rauter
8. Céline thought they should be bayoneting Jews.
9. Petain gave them "certificates of Aryanization."
10. All children under 12 years of age

The Germans Invade Russia (page 27)

1. Purges from 1934 to 1939
2. The mobile killing squads' job was killing Jews.
3. Numbers dropped because Jews had died or left.
4. The elderly and mothers with small children
5. They were forced to jump into a trench.
6. In the river
7. They suffered nightmares, alcoholism, and health problems.
8. Himmler called it a "repulsive duty."
9. Lithuanians burned synagogues and killed Jews.
10. Iasi Jews were left to starve.

Establishing Concentration Camps (page 30)

1. By the time of the French Revolution
2. Labor organizers, political opponents, critics of Nazi policies, and racial "subhumans."
3. To keep farmers from joining the rebels
4. The SA
5. Dachau, Bushenwald, Sachsenhausen
6. Commandant of Dachau
7. He decided whether they lived or died. If they were strong enough, they entered the camp. If not, they were killed.
8. Identification numbers
9. He was a French political prisoner.
10. Gypsies, Jews, and homosexuals

The Major Concentration Camps (page 33)

1. Theodor Eicke
2. 200,000
3. Hanging
4. 25 lashes and 2 weeks of solitary confinement
5. Work makes you free.
6. 5:30 a.m. Black bread and a drink resembling coffee
7. Because the Swedish Red Cross was coming on inspection
8. The Beast of Belsen
9. 1,200 men
10. They carried heavy rocks up a steep slope.

Survival in a Concentration Camp (page 36)

1. The walking dead with blank stares on their faces.
2. Wearing glasses
3. Inmates who had survived a long time in the camp
4. Order and discipline
5. Roll call might last five or six hours, even in freezing cold.
6. Those who reached their limit were killed.
7. The storage place where inmate property was stored
8. Ignore it
9. Food was to be eaten quickly; otherwise, someone would steal it.
10. He or she might be sent to do hard work or be used in a medical experiment.

Murder Becomes Nazi Policy (page 39)

1. "The best and most modern therapy available"
2. Eliminate chronically ill or insane adults
3. Gassed with carbon monoxide
4. The family was given a death certificate and the assurance that every effort to save their loved one had failed.
5. Temporarily stopped the program
6. Nazi euthanasia: person wasn't asked if they wanted to die; Usual: the person asks to die
7. Alcoholism and mental illness
8. Dr. Josef Mengele and Dr. Heinze Thilo
9. Total elimination of Jews
10. Wannsee; Heydrich

Death Camps (page 42)

1. Killing "subhuman" races.
2. The dirty job of body disposal
3. Turnip soup, bread mixed with sawdust, old sausage, and marmalade

4. Inmates dug their own graves, laid in them, and waited to be shot.
5. They were gassed by carbon monoxide in vans.
6. He left bodies out where incoming inmates could see them.
7. 24
8. About 1,000
9. Belzec
10. They were each given 10 ounces of bread.

Auschwitz (page 45)
1. Chosen for its railroad network and abundance of coal
2. Rudolf Hoess
3. Intellectuals, Communists, and Jews
4. Russian POWs
5. 4,756 bodies a day
6. Elderly, mothers with small children, and pregnant women
7. They were given to SS troops and wounded soldiers as Christmas presents.
8. Two days
9. Workers could steal to buy food.
10. Place where prisoners were shot

The Ghettos (page 48)
1. In the Middle Ages
2. Early on the morning they were to move
3. Their property was plundered.
4. There were schools, newspapers, and cultural and religious organizations.
5. People
6. They answered to the Nazis.
7. He tried to do whatever the Germans wanted.
8. Rumkowski told parents to turn them over.
9. He killed himself.
10. Lithuanian anti-Semites

Jewish Resistance (page 51)
1. Because it kept the Nazis from achieving the Final Solution
2. Relocation: being sent to a death camp
3. Partisans: armed groups resisting the German occupation
4. Ustashi: Yugoslav allies of the Nazis
5. Key: made from a mold of the door to the armory
6. Women had smuggled gunpowder to the men involved in the plot.
7. They were afraid the Nazis might make their lives worse.

8. They wanted to go down fighting (or kill Germans).
9. Mordechai Anielewicz
10. They were taken to death camps.

Rescuing Jews (page 54)
1. They might be punished too.
2. To give them time to escape
3. Raoul Wallenberg
4. He passed out official-looking Swedish diplomatic papers to Jews.
5. Secret Jewish investors
6. 1,200
7. Le Chambon
8. Provided hiding places, food, documents, medical care, and arms to Jewish resistance
9. Poland, Greece, and Lithuania
10. Finland

The End of the Camps (page 57)
1. Air raids, Normandy invasion, and Russian advances
2. Hitler wanted to kill Jews faster.
3. Wanted 10,000 trucks, coffee, sugar, tea, and soap
4. They saw it as an attempt to split the Alliance (by using trucks only against the Russians, Stalin would have interpreted that as a deal made behind his back).
5. Wanted Birkenau completely destroyed so no trace remained
6. Figures: four million (two-thirds of six million)
7. Evidence: records, bodies, and piles of eyeglasses, shoes, and hair
8. The children who were there
9. Bradley: the smell of death
10. Civilians: Many were shocked and some fainted.

The Day of Judgment: Nuremberg (page 60)
1. They were given dignified funerals.
2. He took poison.
3. As an SS enlisted man
4. Francis Biddle and Robert Jackson
5. Crimes against humanity (fourth category)
6. 1.5 million
7. 12
8. He had direct orders.
9. Argentina; Israelis
10. He was never captured.

Zionism Fulfilled: The Birth of Israel (page 63)
1. Theodor Herzl
2. Five million
3. To the nation of their birth
4. Displaced person
5. Many were killed or injured by anti-Semitic mobs.
6. *Balfour Declaration*
7. 75,000
8. Arabs
9. Truman
10. 1948

Could the Holocaust Have Been Avoided? (page 66)
1. The Depression: It is as easy to be hungry at home.
2. Giving in to demands
3. Evian
4. German Jews going to Cuba
5. They were refused entry.
6. Eighty percent opposed changing them.
7. Long said Communists and Nazis might sneak in.
8. Secretary of Treasury Morgenthau
9. Bomb railways, crematoria, and gas chambers at Auschwitz
10. Arab oil producers

Vocabulary Answers

(page 69)
1. Prejudice: a judgment or opinion formed before the facts are known; unreasonable bias
2. Discrimination: a showing of partiality or prejudice in treatment; specifically, action or policies directed against the welfare of minority groups
3. Racism: a doctrine or teaching, without scientific support, that claims to find racial differences in character, intelligence, etc., that asserts the superiority of one race over another or others, and that seeks to maintain the supposed purity of a race or the races
4. Persecution: constant harassment designed to injure or distress; cruel oppression, especially for reasons of religion, politics, or race
5. Apathy: lack of emotion; lack of interest; unconcern; indifference
6. Genocide: the systematic killing of, or a program of action intended to destroy, a whole national or ethnic group

(Application to the Holocaust and modern examples will vary.)

Bibliography

Hundreds of books have been written about the Holocaust. Like any subject, the student beginning research needs to start with broader books and articles, look at the index or the footnotes, and see where that author found his or her material. Some books dealing with the Holocaust may be too graphic for younger students, so the teacher needs to provide guidance.

Reference books

Encyclopedia Judaica. (Jerusalem: Keter, 1973).

Encyclopedia of Jewish History. (New York: Facts on File, 1986).

Gilbert, Martin. *Atlas of the Holocaust.* (New York: Da Capo, 1982).

Gutman, Israel. *Encyclopedia of the Holocaust.* (New York: Macmillan, 1990).

New Standard Jewish Encyclopedia. (New York: Facts on File, 1992).

Snyder, Louis. *Encyclopedia of the Third Reich.* (New York: Paragon, 1976).

Zentner, Christian and Bedürftig, Friedemann (eds.). *The Encyclopedia of the Third Reich.* (New York: Macmillan, 1991).

Pre-Holocaust sources

Carr, William. *A History of Germany 1815–1990.* (London: Edward Arnold, 1991).

Halperin, S. William. *Germany Tried Democracy.* (New York: Thomas Cromwell, 1946).

Hitler, Adolf. *Mein Kampf.* (New York: Reynal & Hitchcock, 1939).

Katz, Jacob. *From Prejudice to Destruction, Anti-Semitism, 1700–1933.* (New York: Hart, 1965).

Langsam, Walter. *Documents and Readings in the History of Europe Since 1918.* (Chicago: Lippincott, 1939).

May, Arthur. *Europe and the Two World Wars.* (New York: Scribner's, 1947).

Nazism 1919–1945 (2 vols.). (New York: Schocken, 1984).

Sachar, Abram. *A History of the Jews.* (New York: Knopf, 1958).

Valentin, Veit. *The German People.* (New York: Knopf, 1946).

Young, Peter (ed.). *The Marshall Cavendish Illustrated Encyclopedia of World War I.* (New York: Marshall Cavendish, 1986).

Hitler and Nazi Germany

Allen, William. *The Nazi Seizure of Power: The Experience of a Single German Town.* (New York: Franklin Watts, 1973).

Breitman, Richard. *The Architect of Genocide: Himmler and the Final Solution.* (New York: Knopf, 1991).

Bullock, Alan. *Hitler: a Study in Tyranny.* (New York: Harper & Row, 1962).

Kershaw, Ian. *Profiles in Power—Hitler.* (London: Longman Group, 1991).

Noakes, J. and Pridham, G. (eds.). *Nazism: A History in Documents and Eyewitness Accounts, 1919–1945* (2 vols.). (New York: Schocken, 1984).

Schleunes, Karl. *The Twisted Road to Auschwitz.* (Urbana: University of Illinois, 1970).

Shirer, William. *The Rise and Fall of the Third Reich.* (New York: Simon and Schuster, 1960).

Snyder, Louis. *Encyclopedia of the Third Reich.* (New York: Paragon, 1976).

Speer, Albert. *Inside the Third Reich.* (New York: Avon, 1971).

Zentner, Christian and Bedürftig, Friedemann (editors). *The Encyclopedia of the Third Reich.* (New York: Macmillan, 1991).

Holocaust

Abzug, Robert. *Inside the Vicious Heart: Americans and the Liberation of Nazi Concentration Camps.* (New York: Oxford, 1985).

Arad, Yitzak. *The Pictorial History of the Holocaust.* (New York: Macmillan, 1990).

Bailey, Ronald. *Prisoners of War.* (Alexandria, Virginia: Time-Life, 1981).

Bartoszewski, Wladyslaw. *Warsaw Death Ring.* (New York: Interpress, 1968).

Berenbaum, Michael. *The World Must Know.* (Boston: Little Brown, 1993).

Czech, Danuta. *Auschwitz Chronicle.* (New York: Henry Holt, 1990).

Dawidowicz, Lucy. *The War Against the Jews.* (New York: Holt, Rinehart & Winston, 1975).

de Lange, Nicholas. *Atlas of the Jewish World.* (New York: Facts on File, 1992).

Donat, Alexander. *The Holocaust Kingdom.* (New York: Holocaust Library, 1978).

Flenders, Harold. *Rescue in Denmark.* (New York: Holocaust Library, 1978).

Fogelman, Eva. *Conscience and Courage: Rescuers of Jews During the Holocaust.* (New York: Doubleday, 1994).

Frank, Anne. *The Diary of a Young Girl.* (New York: Bantam, 1991).

Fried, Hedi. *The Road to Auschwitz: Fragments of a Life.* (Lincoln: University of Nebraska, 1996).

Gilbert, Martin. *The Holocaust: A History of the Jews During the Second World War.* (New York: Holt, Rinehart & Winston, 1985).

Grunberger, Richard. *Hitler's SS.* (New York: Dorset, 1970).

Gutman, Ysrael. *The Jews of Warsaw.* (Bloomington: Indiana University, 1982).

Hallie, Phillip. *Lest Innocent Blood Be Shed, the Story of Le Chambon and How Goodness Happened There.* (New York: Harper, 1979).

Heydecker, Joe and Leeb, Johannes. *The Nuremberg Trials.* (London: Heinemann, 1962).

Hilberg, Raul. *The Destruction of the European Jews.* (New York: Octagon, 1978).

Isocovici, Salomon. *Man of Ashes.* (Lincoln: University of Nebraska, 1997).

Korczak, Janus. *Ghetto Diary.* (New York: Holocaust Library, 1978).

Langer, Lawrence. *Holocaust Testimonies.* (New Haven, CT: Yale, 1991).

Levi, Primo. *Survival in Auschwitz.* (New York: Collier, 1993).

Levin, Nora. *The Holocaust: The Destruction of European Jewry 1933–1945.* (New York: Schocken, 1973).

Lewin, Rhoda (ed.) *Witnesses to the Holocaust.* New York: Twayne, 1990).

Lifton, Robert. *The Nazi Doctors.* (New York: Harper-Collins, 1986).

Lipstadt, Deborah. *Denying the Holocaust.* Jerusalem: Plume, 1994.

Lustig, Arnost. *Children of the Holocaust.* (Evanston, IL: Northwestern University, 1986).

Marrus, Michael. *Vichy France and the Jews.* (New York: Basic Books, 1981).

Mosley, Leonard. *The Reich Marshal: A Biography of Hermann Goering.* (Garden City, New York: Doubleday, 1974).

Persico, Joseph. *Nuremberg: Infamy on Trial.* (New York: Penguin, 1994).

Pogonowski, Iwo. *Jews in Poland.* (New York: Hippocrene, 1993).

Pryce-Jones, David. *Paris in the Third Reich.* (New York: Holt Rinehart & Winston, 1981).

Rossel, Seymour. *The Holocaust: The World and the Jews 1933–1945.* West Orange, NJ: Behrman House, 1992.

Steiner, Jean-Francois. *Treblinka.* (New York: New American Library, 1979).

Tec, Nechama. *When Light Pierced the Darkness: Christian Rescue of Jews in Poland.* (New York: Oxford, 1986).

ten Boom, Corrie. *The Hiding Place.* (Minneapolis: World Wide, 1971).

Trunk, Isaiah. *Judenrat, The Jewish Councils in Eastern Europe under Nazi Occupation.* (Lincoln: University of Nebraska, 1996).

Tusa, Ann and John. *The Nuremberg Trial.* (New York: Atheneum, 1986).

Wiesel, Elie. *Night.* (New York: Bantam, 1982).

Yahil, Leni. *The Holocaust.* (New York: Oxford, 1990).

Zuccotti, Susan. *The Italians and the Holocaust. (New York: Basic Books, 1987).*